TOP **10**
CORSICA

W0113948

CONTENTS

44

Top 10 of Everything

78

Area by Area

106

Streetsmart

CORSICA

INTRODUCING

Scenic road winding past the Calanques de Piana

WELCOME TO
CORSICA

With its historic towns, superb Mediterranean dishes and epic ancient monuments – not to mention those mountains and beaches – Corsica is made for adventurers. Don't want to miss a thing? With Top 10 Corsica, you'll enjoy the very best the island has to offer.

"L'Île de Beauté" (the Isle of Beauty) is fully deserving of its nickname. Few islands combine sea and summit so dramatically, with the highest peaks in the Mediterranean plunging to meet waters teeming with marine life. The island has been whittled over eons into two soaring mountain ranges, marked by jagged features like the Calanques de Piana and traversed by Europe's toughest hiking route, the infamous GR20. Off the coast, Corsica offers some of the finest sailing in Europe, and the island's jagged inlets and echoing caves are best explored by boat.

Admiring the sea from Capo di Muro

When all that adventuring gets too much, you're never far from one of France's most beautiful beaches. The golden sands of Palombaggia or the quiet coves near Calvi are the perfect place to kick back in the sunshine, perhaps with a local wine in hand.

While Corsica is a haven for lovers of the outdoors, it's not all mountain peaks and rugged hikes. In historic towns like Bastia, Bonifacio and Corte, you'll find examples of Corsica's thriving independent culture: food festivals celebrate a unique mix of Italian and French cuisines, local musicians practise polyphonic singing, and a plethora of religious traditions speak of Corsica's long Catholic past. The birthplace of Napoleon Bonaparte has a proud history as varied as the meats on its charcuterie boards, with a story stretching back to the Neolithic peoples of Filitosa. And speaking of Napoleon, you'll find the legacy of the French Emperor writ large across his birthplace, Ajaccio, today the island's bustling capital and largest city.

So, where to start? With Top 10 Corsica, of course. This pocket-sized guide gets to the heart of the island with simple lists of 10, expert local knowledge and comprehensive maps, helping you turn an ordinary trip into an extraordinary one.

THE STORY OF
CORSICA

Corsica has been controlled by a plethora of powerful rulers throughout its long history – including the Phoenicians, Romans, Genoese and French – who each contributed to the island's unique cultural identity. Here's the story of how it came to be.

Corsica Begins

It's thought that human settlement on Corsica began around 10,000 BCE, but one of the earliest pieces of human evidence dates from roughly 7500 BCE: the Araguina-Sennola skeleton was discovered near Bonifacio and is now known as the "Lady of Bonifacio".

In the 5th century BCE, Phoenician settlers founded Aléria, south of Bastia. Inspired by Corsica's rich, mountainous terrain, they named the island as a whole "Kallistè", meaning beautiful. They were to rule in peace for a few centuries, until the Romans set their sights on the island.

Roman intervention began around 225 BCE, but it took their armies almost a century – and 10 military expeditions – to conquer Corsica, due to the island's famously rugged terrain and the defensive strategies of the Phoenicians. Once established, the Romans stayed for almost 700 years.

Invasions and Illness

After the decline of the Roman Empire, everyone wanted a piece of Corsica, and the island was subject to raids from invaders including the Goths, Byzantines and Vandals. In 754, feudal lords (many of them Tuscan or Ligurian) intervened in this power struggle, carving up the island before passing control to the Pope and the Kingdom of Pisa. Under Pisan influence, Corsicans began to build churches and residential parishes.

The Pisan era was marked by frequent skirmishes with the Genoese, however. By 1187, Genoa had taken possession of Bonifacio and, in 1268,

Corsican revolutionaries in battle with the French

Louis XV, who oversaw France's victory at Ponte-Novo

founded the city of Calvi. Following the Battle of Meloria in 1284, the Genoese took control of the whole island – they built vast citadelles and dotted the coast with towers, while their trade ushered in a period of great wealth.

In the Middle Ages, frequent comings-and-goings by boat meant Corsica became a hotspot for diseases. When the Black Death swept across Europe in the mid-1300s, two thirds of the island was wiped out. The last recorded case of bubonic plague in Corsica was as recent as 1945.

Independence Struggles

In the 1400s, the French launched a wave of invasions in an attempt to gain a foothold in the Mediterranean. Genoese power was swiftly reinstated, but Corsicans became increasingly disenchanted with their rulers. After new taxes were imposed in the 18th century, a series of revolts were to change the course of the island's history. In 1745, Corsican politician Jean-Pierre Gaffori became the leader of a major insurrection, followed by 30-year-old political leader Pascal Paoli in 1755. Paoli succeeded in establishing a constitutional state and created a local army. For just 14 years, the island was proudly independent under Paoli's rule. The period came to an end with the French regaining control of Corsica after their victory in the battle of Ponte-Novo.

Moments in History

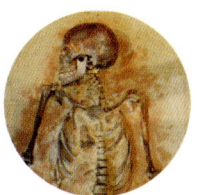

7500 BCE
The 1972 discovery of the "Lady of Bonifacio" dates concrete evidence of human life in Corsica.

754
After the fall of Rome, numerous powers vie for control. In 754 CE, Corsica is pledged to the Kingdom of Pisa.

1284
Genoese fleets beat the Pisans to take control of Corsica, a control they retain for almost 500 years.

1755
Pascal Paoli is elected head of the resistance and declares an independent Corsica, creating a new constitution and universal suffrage.

1768-9
Genoa asks the King of France, Louis XV, for help in reclaiming Corsica. France annexes the island, claiming it as its own.

1794–6
Aided by the British, Paoli attempts to reclaim Corsica from the French. They are unsuccessful, and Paoli returns to exile.

1914–18
Corsica suffers heavier losses than any other French region during WWI, losing more than a third of its soldiers.

1943
Corsica becomes the first French region to regain independence from occupying Nazi forces.

1967
The Simeoni brothers found the nationalist ARC party (Action for Rebirth of Corsica), the predecessor of the island's current nationalist party.

2018–2024
Pè a Corsica, a nationalist coalition,is the majority party. The Corsican language undergoes a resurgence, and progress is made in the movement for the island's full political autonomy.

Napoleon in Corsica in the early 19th century

A French Corsica

Sentenced to death by French revolutionaries, the Jacobins, Pascal Paoli appealed to the English for help in taking Corsica back. English intervention led to the birth of the brief Anglo-Corsican kingdom (1794–6), but in 1796, French troops were sent out to retake the island. They were led by a young and soon-to-be infamous Corsican-born officer, Napoleon Bonaparte.

After Napoleon's fall in 1815, the 19th century in Corsica was one of relative calm under French rule. A secure economy and a wave of infra-structural development ushered in an era of peace, while in the late 19th century, Corsica's tourism industry developed. The Industrial Revolution saw a period of decline, however, as the island relied on agriculture and lagged behind the developing mainland.

War and Independence

Despite improvements in living standards, dire poverty afflicted the island in the early 20th century, forcing thousands of Corsicans to emigrate. During World War II, Mussolini's forces conquered Corsica, but the Italians were met with heavy resistance from locals, and in 1943 Corsica became the first French territory to become liberated from Fascist control, a huge boost for Allied forces.

As the war came to an end, the many Corsicans who had gone abroad were repatriated and there were renewed calls for Corsican autonomy led by a new party, the Front Régionaliste Corse (FRC). The FRC, together with the Action Régionaliste Corse (ARC), demanded full political control for Corsica, a decentralized government and protection for Corsican land. The independence movement was punctuated by occasional acts of political violence throughout the 1960s and 1970s. This violence might have abated, but the nationalist movement remains very much alive, with progress made in the pursuit of sovereignty.

Locals demonstrating for Corsican independence in 1975

Corsica Today

In 2018, Corsica was granted the status of *collectivité territoriale unique* (single territorial collectivity), which gives the island more legislative powers than other regions of France. Since 2015, Corsica's governing party has been Pè a Corsica (For Corsica), a nationalist party formed by a coalition of Femu a Corsica and Corsica Libera. The Corsican language, Corsu, which went into decline in the mid-20th century, is undergoing a revival (39 per cent of the population now speak Corsu as well as French). Tourism remains the island's key industry, though Corsica is also home to a world renowned food scene that attracts crowds of global visitors.

Ajaccio, one of Corsica's main tourist hubs

TOP 10
EXPERIENCES

Planning the perfect trip to Corsica? Whether you're visiting for the first time or making a return trip, there are some things you simply shouldn't miss out on. To make the most of your time – and to enjoy the very best this incredible island has to offer – be sure to add these experiences to your list.

1 Hit the beach
The custard-coloured beaches of the Désert des Agriate (p57) aren't the easiest to access, but that's what keeps them so perfect. You can reach them by boat, and numerous companies run a water taxi service from St-Florent (p36), or you can take a mountain bike from Casta.

2 Time travel in Bonifacio
Perched on high cliffs in the verdant south, the fort town of Bonifacio looks straight over the sea to the Italian island of Sardinia. Bonifacio's old town is still completely fortified, its oldest part built in the 12th century, when Corsica was still under Pisan rule.

3 Hike the GR20
Europe's toughest trek certainly lives up to its reputation. The 180-km- (110-mile-) long GR20 (p62) isn't for the faint-hearted, with tricky scrambles and knee-busting climbs (plus some truly epic views). Many complete the entire route, but you could just try one section.

4 Marvel at marine life
The Réserve Naturelle de Scandola is a protected marine park defined by its soaring red cliffs, with dramatic rust-coloured pillars and caves lapped by azure waters. Accessible only by boat from Calvi or Porto, the reserve is one of the island's most striking natural landscapes.

5 Sample local charcuterie

In Corsica, there are more varieties of cheese and charcuterie than you can shake a stick at. The island's specialities include *coppa* (pig shoulder), *figatellu* (a Corsican liver sausage), prosciutto and the creamy goats' cheese, *brocciu*.

6 Hit the road

The hairpin bends may be intimidating, but driving in Corsica is spectacular. Drive the west coast of Cap Corse (p34), where a rollercoaster road winds from mausoleums clinging to cliffs to storm-ravaged beaches and soaring granite pinnacles.

7 Island hop

Tiny islands pepper the wild coast, each so small they make Corsica itself seem like a continent. The Îles Lavezzi (p89) are splintered between Corsica and Sardinia, while the lush Îles Sanguinaires (p22) are strung out from Ajaccio on the west coast.

8 Explore rural living

For a true flavour of the island, travel to its rural interior. The little town of Quenza (p92) and the nearby villages are the perfect places to take life slowly, as you soak up the crisp mountain air. The hikes in the interior are also among the island's wildest.

9 Ride the rails

U Trinighellu, or "the little train" (p39), isn't the fastest way to see the island, but it may be the prettiest. Running between Ajaccio and either Calvi or Bastia, it goes through 32 tunnels and over 52 bridges, and took some 20,000 workers to create.

10 Get high

Corte (p40) was chosen by Pascal Paoli to be the capital of independent Corsica. Once the island was conquered by the French, Ajaccio was named the capital, but Corte still has the island's only university, and an excellent museum of Corsican history.

ITINERARIES

Hopping from beach to beach, discovering Genoese forts or enjoying a cold Pietra beer: there's a lot to see and do in Corsica. With places to eat, drink and hike, these itineraries offer ways to spend 2 days and 5 days on the island.

2 DAYS IN BONIFACIO

Day 1

Morning
Grab your hire car from either Figari Airport or Porto-Vecchio's port *(p89)* and head to the clifftop town of Bonifacio. If you're driving anything larger than a soapbox (recommended given the steepness of the hills), park outside the old town – the roads aren't wide enough to swing a cat. Spend the morning exploring the old town, which dates from the 9th century and was founded as a stronghold against Saracen raids. Grab coffee and a slice of *fiadone* (a semi-sweet cake made with sheep's cheese and vanilla) from Café des Vestiges *(3 Rue du Portone)* to enjoy perched on the ramparts of the medieval citadelle. You'll be sitting atop tall cliffs, flanked by buildings that lean slightly like a jauntily angled

> ☕ **DRINK**
> Drive out to Domaine Zuria *(domainezuria.com)*, a family-run vineyard with sea views near Bonifacio, to enjoy a tasting and a tour of their extensive wine cellars.

beret. In most weather, the views over to Sardinia are simply spectacular.

Afternoon
It's a 30-km (18-mile) drive to Palombaggia *(p90)*, a crescent moon of fine, cream-coloured sand that regularly tops lists as Corsica's best beach (and competition is stiff). Hire a paddleboard from the I Pini rental outlet (found on the beach) to admire the beach from the water. Most of the hilly backdrop is covered by tangled foliage, and what buildings there are

Bonifacio perched on its rocky promontory

are well camouflaged. It looks like a desert island, with smooth boulders peppering the almost translucent water. Enjoy dinner at Palm Beach (*lepalmbeachpalombaggia.com/en*) – its wood-fired pizzas are particularly good – with your toes in the sand, before heading back to Bonifacio.

Day 2

Morning
Enjoy a lazy morning with a leisurely coffee and croissant from Pâtisserie Sorba (*3 Rue Saint-Dominique*) – you'll get plenty of exercise this afternoon. Refreshed, wander around Bonifacio's galleries and artisanal shops; make sure you spend time in Les Terrasses d'Aragon (*lesterrassesdaragon.com*), one of the island's finest makers of bespoke penknives. Making intricate knives has been a Corsican artisanal tradition stretching back to the early years of Roman occupation.

Afternoon
It's time to tackle the coastal path east. The route is 7 km (14 miles) there-and-back, and leads past striking rock formations with superb coastal views. The path is generally straightforward, although not always well marked, so it's worth having a map as back-up. You're heading towards the incredible cave of Grotte Saint Antoine, where erosion has created a natural, circular skylight – you can perch on the rocks and watch the waves ebb and flow from above. Time your walk back to admire the sunset over Bonifacio, and enjoy a fine Corsican meal at Cantina Doria (*p93*).

> ### ✂ EAT
> When the sea is all around you, you know the seafood is fresh. La Minute Moule (*Rue des Moulins, 20169*) is a real institution for *moules frites* (mussels and French fries), with fine views over the port.

Ersa
Macinaggio
5
Luri
Baratelli
CAR
CAR
Albo
Marine
de Sisco
Golfe de
St-Florent
Nonza
Miomo
WATER TAXI
Bastia
Mediterranean
Sea
Désert des
Agriates
Lotu
3 **4**
CAR
St-Florent
Saleccia
Curzo
Monetta
Étang di
Biguglia
Palumbare
Beach
1
Lama
Calvi
2
Borgo
Poretta
Sainte-
Catherine
BOAT
Argentella
Ponte Leccia
Grotte Saint
Antoine
Haut-Asco
Piedicroce
Scandola Nature Reserve
Girolata
Sovéria

0 kilometres   15
0 miles   15

Calanques of Piana

5 DAYS IN CORSICA

Day 1

Kick-off your time in Calvi by spending the morning languidly pottering around the 18th-century Citadelle (*p38*). Many small stores display fine artisanal wares, with craftspeople using local and salvaged materials to create everything from jewellery to furniture. Once you've had your fill of shopping, head to Calvi Beach (*p38*) to relax, and keep an ear out for U Trinighellu, Corsica's little train.

This afternoon, take a boat trip to Scandola Nature Reserve (*p54*) and the Calanques de Piana. Corsica's only UNESCO-listed reserve is home to caves of volcanic rock, crystal-clear water and astonishing marine bio-diversity. Most trips stop at Girolata (*p58*), a small hamlet with a handful of bars in which to enjoy a cold Pietra

Genoese watchtower above the sea near Girolata

beer. Cows wander freely along a palm-fronded beach, with a fudge-coloured fort on the headland. Most boat trips from Calvi last half a day, leaving you with time for a drink and a small bite to eat at Marco Plage (*Route de la plage, Calvi*).

SHOP
Stop at OSL Corsica (osl-corsica.com) in St-Florent to pick up jewellery decorated with the island's distinctive shell, known as the Eye of St Lucia.

Day 2

Drive east to St-Florent (p36). It may be under 70 km (45 miles), but this is a road trip worth taking time over. The first half of the drive is littered with secluded beaches, such as Palumbare Beach, perfect for a mid-journey dip, with goat tracks leading to Genoese watchtowers. The second hour is nothing short of spectacular, a helter-skelter of twists and turns that cuts above the Désert des Agriate (p103). In St-Florent, soak up the atmosphere at Bar Le Passage (Bar Le Passage, 20217). Overlooking the square, it's at its most atmospheric in the early evening, when locals crowd the area to play *boules*.

Day 3

Reserve a boat trip going to both Saleccia and Lotu beaches, and opt for the smaller "water taxis" over the monster steamers. In a half-day package, the boat drops you at Saleccia Beach (p56) and picks you up from Lotu, leaving you with either a 45-minute inland walk or 90-minute coastal walk between the two. The sand at both is as soft as a carpet and the colour of custard, and it's not hard to see why they regularly vie for Corsica's "best beach". Food options are limited, so pack your own picnic. Upon your return, treat yourself to a pastry or maquis-flavoured gelato from La Gelateria de Saint-Florent in the town centre.

Day 4

It's road trip time. Drive along the west coast of Cap Corse, a journey of hairpin bends, which plummets and rises between hilltop villages and stone beaches – both the views and the driving are heart in mouth stuff. Your first stop will be in the pretty village of Nonza (p104). Have lunch at O'Lamparo (olamparo restaurant.fr) to enjoy the panoramic views, before cutting across inland to the port town of Macinaggio (p34) for the night.

Day 5

After a leisurely morning swim, head in the direction of Porticciolo. At the organic vineyard of Terra di Catoni (terradicatoni.com), you can take a tour of the vines before tasting some of the island's finest wines. Then, it's only a short drive to Bastia (p32), your final stop. Take a walk through the old town to learn how it grew from a humble fishing village under Genoese rule. You can wander alongside the renovated seaside walkway before enjoying a meal at Le Mademoiselle (lemade moisellebastia.fr). Catch the ferry back to the mainland from Bastia.

The port of Bastia in the early evening

TOP 10 HIGHLIGHTS

Boats moored in St-Florent

EXPLORE THE
HIGHLIGHTS

There are some sights in Corsica that you simply shouldn't miss, and it's these attractions that make the Top 10. Discover what makes each one a must-see on the following pages.

L'Île-Rousse

Calvi **8**

Calenzana

Argentella

Partinello Calasima

10 Golfe de Porto

Piana

Guagno

Cargèse

Golfe de Sagone Tiuccia

Ucciani

Ajaccio **1** Bastelicaccia

Portigliolo

Casalabriva

Golfe de Valinco **2**

Le Sartenais **3**

Tizzano

Mediterranean Sea

0 kilometres   10
0 miles   10

Cap Corse **6**

Luri

Albo

Erbalunga

St-Florent and the Nebbio **7**

Bastia **5**

Lama

Borgo

Asco

Ponte Leccia

Folelli

Sovéria

San Nicolo

Corte **9**

Spazzola

Vivario

Bocognano

Poggio di Nazza

Aléria

Ghisonaccia

Zicavo

Travo

Aullène

Favone

Carbini

Pinarello

Montagne de Cagna

Porto-Vecchio

Tyrrhenian Sea

Bonifacio **4**

1 Ajaccio

2 Golfe de Valinco

3 Le Sartenais

4 Bonifacio

5 Bastia

6 Cap Corse

7 St-Florent and the Nebbio

8 Calvi

9 Corte and its Hinterland

10 Golfe del Porto

AJACCIO

📍 H3 ℹ️ 3 Blvd du Roi Jérôme; ajaccio-tourisme.com

With a backdrop of granite mountains and azure sea, Ajaccio ranks among the most splendid capitals in the Mediterranean. Travellers from English artist Edward Lear to French writer Guy de Maupassant were enthralled by its setting, and the imperial city remains an essential stop for visitors – not least because of its association with Napoleon Bonaparte, who was born here.

1 Lazaret Ollandini

🏠 Quartier Aspretto
🌐 lelazaret-ollandini.com

Located about halfway along the coastal road to the airport, this former quarantine station is now a performance venue. It hosts operas and concerts, and contains the Marc Petit Museum, which features art exhibitions.

2 Îles Sanguinaires

One of the lovely short stories in French novelist Alphonse Daudet's famous collections *Lettres de mon Moulin*, was inspired by a visit to this archipelago of islets, which taper into the sea.

3 Fishing Harbour

Ajaccio's tiny fishing quay, just south of the marina, is a great place to visit early in the morning, when the night's catch is being landed against a backdrop of palms, yachts and giant ferries

4 Ajaccio Cathedral

Dedicated to the Virgin Mary, this late Baroque cathedral features a painting by Eugène Delacroix of the Virgin holding the Sacred Heart. In 1771, Napoleon was baptized here.

Central nave of Ajaccio's cathedral

The town and marina of Ajaccio

EAT
Le Don Quichotte *(p87)* is a great spot for sampling traditional Corsican desserts. It also serves excellent local fish and delicious seafood.

---

5 Open-Air Food Market

Every morning during the summer months, local producers descend on Place Foch (also known as Place des Palmiers), in front of the town hall, to sell artisanal food.

6 Citadelle

Originally built by the Genoese, this hexagonal citadel juts into the bay next to St-François beach. The fortress played a key role in history, holding captive resistance fighters in World War II.

7 Maison Bonaparte

P3 Rue St Charles
Hours vary, chech website musees-nationaux-malmaison.fr

The Bonaparte family lived here until Paolist rebels drove them into exile in 1793. The rooms feature personal possessions of the family. Don't miss the famed sofa on which Napoleon was born.

8 Les Milelli

Nestled in an olive grove, Les Milelli was the Bonapartes' country retreat. Napoleon stayed here during his last visit to Ajaccio in 1799. The grounds make for an excellent picnic spot.

9 Salon Napoléonien

P2 ajaccio.fr

Napoleon's death mask is among the quirky memorabilia on show at this small museum inside the Hôtel de Ville on Place Foch.

10 Palais Fesch

P1 50–52 Rue Cardinal Fesch
May–Oct: 9:15am–6pm daily; Nov–Apr: 9am–5pm daily
1 Jan, 25 Dec
musee-fesch.com

This museum houses a fine collection of Renaissance and Baroque art *(p24)*. Highlights of the collection include *Leda and the Swan*, a 16th-century painting by Paolo Veronese.

NAPOLEON AND CORSICA

Born in Ajaccio, Napoleon spent his formative years in Paris, becoming a deeply passionate advocate of the French Revolution, which did little to endear him to Pascal Paoli's nationalist regime back home. Having been chased into exile by Paoli's fervent supporters, Napoleon shunned his homeland for good, returning only once, very briefly, while en route to France after his Egyptian campaign. His legacy on the island remains complex.

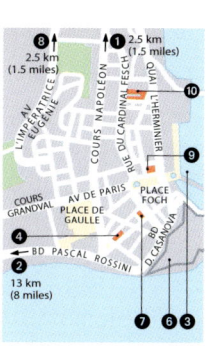

Bust of Napoleon, Maison Bonaparte

Palais Fesch – Musée des Beaux Arts

1. Gaulli's Joseph Recites a Dream to His Brothers

Also known as Il Baciccio, Giovanni Battista Gaulli (1639–1709) was Bernini's protégé and a veteran of the Baroque style. This painting is presented in the museum's large gallery next to its companion piece, *Joseph Recognised by His Brothers*. The subject of these pieces is taken from the Old Testament.

2. Botticelli's Virgin and Child with an Angel

Virgin and Child with an Angel is one of the finest pictures painted by Sandro Botticelli (1445–1510), a great master of the early Renaissance. The Virgin's open display of affection makes the painting one of the loveliest works in the museum.

3. Titian's Portrait of a Man with a Glove

The jewel in the crown of the Palais Fesch collection is this exquisite portrait by legendary Venetian artist Titian (c 1488–1576). Here, he limits the colours he uses and darkens the background, focusing in on the hands and expression of the sitter to create a sense of psychological presence.

4. Tommaso's Mystical Marriage of St Catherine

The figure kneeling in the foreground here is St Catherine of Alexandria, who is said to have had a vision in which Christ took her as his spiritual bride in the presence of the Virgin Mary. It is a fine example of early Renaissance art by Niccolò di Tommaso (c 1346–76).

5. Bernini's Portrait of David

One of the masters of the Italian Baroque, Gianlorenzo Bernini (1598–1680) enjoyed an illustrious career as a sculptor and architect. He was also an exceptional portrait painter, and sometimes worked with his followers, as in this brooding, psychologically intense work.

6. Veronese's Leda and the Swan

This erotic painting by Paolo Veronese (1528–88) depicts a scene from Greek mythology in which Zeus seduces Leda (the mother of Helen of Troy). It is prized for its subject matter, a recurrent motif in Renaissance paintings.

7. Gérard's Napoleon in Coronation Robes

François Gérard (1770–1837) painted all the renowned figures of the Napoleonic period in France, especially the recently crowned emperor, who is shown here in full regalia. The work is the highlight of the museum's Napoleonic collection.

Botticelli's *Virgin and Child with an Angel* (c 1465–67)

The Departure of Rebecca (c 1710) by Francesco Solimena

8. Solimena's The Departure of Rebecca

Francesco Solimena (1657–1747) was one of the most prolific and successful figures of the Baroque period, and his strength lay in the creation of dramatic biblical scenes filled with movement and vivid detail. *The Departure of Rebecca* depicts the poignant moment when Rebecca leaves her home to marry Isaac, the son of Abraham. It's a stunning example of the artist's pioneering command of light and shadow, and rich palette.

9. Recco's Still Life with Fish and Lobster

This remarkable piece of work is by Neapolitan artist Giuseppe Recco (1634–95), who is known for his exceptional talent in depicting everyday objects with stunning realism. Few visitors can pass this captivating still life without pausing to admire its truly incredible photo-realisitic quality.

10. Tura's Virgin Mary and Child with St Jerome and a Holy Martyr

A beautiful 15th-century painting by the Italian painter Cosmè Tura of Ferrara (c 1433–95), this was part of the impressive collection bequeathed by Cardinal Joseph Fesch to the city of Ajaccio in 1839.

A CARDINAL'S COLLECTION

Cardinal Joseph Fesch, Napoleon's step-uncle, amassed the world's largest private collection of art – around 16,000 pieces spanning five centuries – during a time when Europe's art markets were flooded with plundered works. While most of the Cardinal's estate was left to Napoleon's family after his death in 1839, he bequeathed 1,500 pieces to Ajaccio. However, Fesch's principal heir, Napoleon's elder brother, contested this bequest, and the family sold off the bulk of the estate before the legal case was resolved. Masterpieces from the collection can now be seen in many of the national galleries in Europe.

GOLFE DE VALINCO

H5   21 Av Napoléon III, Propriano; lacorsedesorigines.com

The most southerly of the four great gulfs indenting Corsica's west coast, Valinco presents an arresting spectacle when seen from the high, panoramic ridges enfolding it. Its vivid blue waters seamlessly cleave into the heart of the Alta Rocca region, where picturesque orange-roofed settlements cling to hillsides that are covered in verdant holm-oak forest and dense, impenetrable maquis.

TOP TIP

The Genoese Tour di Capo Neru (stone tower) is on the western tip of Golfe de Valinco.

1 Filitosa
The prehistoric settlement of Filitosa (p46) is renowned for its collection of carved standing stones. Its eerily defiant features were chiselled from granite 5,000 years ago.

2 Campomoro
Spread behind a shell-shaped bay overlooked by a watch-tower, the small village of Campomoro, on the south coast of the Golfe de Valinco, is a quiet and secluded spot.

3 Porto-Pollo
This fishing village serves as the region's scuba-diving hub, as well as a base for trips to hidden beaches.

4 Propriano
A tranquil village during the off-season, Propriano transforms into a lively resort and ferry port in the summer months, thanks to its many beaches and coves. Visitors flock to the

Lighthouse in the harbour at Propriano

stylish waterfront café terraces lining the town's marina to enjoy the coastal views.

5 Gulf Cruises

w promenades-en-mer-propriano.fr
Excursion boats leave daily from Propriano Marina in the summer, calling at several coves, snorkelling hot spots and photogenic rock formations only reachable by sea. Some outfits offer sunset cruises as well.

6 Ste-Lucie de Tallano

Bucolic olive and almond groves surround this picturesque Alta Rocca village (p89). Taste cold-pressed oil in a mill outlet, or watch *pétanque* players on a plane-shaded square.

7 Plage de Cupabia

Valinco's loveliest beach is the place to sidestep the summer crowds. Hidden over the hill from Porto-Pollo, it lies beyond the range of day-tripping Ajaccians, in a gloriously wild setting.

8 Col de Siu

An unforgettable drive inland from Propriano, along the little-used D557, leads to this remote and tranquil mountain pass which is visited by more goats than people. Scramble over the rocks for magnificent views of the gulf.

9 Fozzano

This village is famous as the home of the real-life heroine who inspired French writer Prosper Mérimée's vendetta novel *Colomba*. Its granite tower houses recall the conflicts that beset the region in the 1800s.

10 Bains de Caldane

☑ K5 ☑ D148 Rte de Granacce, Ste-Lucie de Tallano ☑ 9am–8pm daily ☑
One of Valinco's quirkier attractions is this tiny hot spring, situated just 6 km (4 miles) from Ste-Lucie de Tallano.

CORSICAN VENDETTAS

Corsica is infamous for the long-standing blood feuds that arose as part of a strict social code: it was customary to kill anyone who wronged one's family honor. The appearance of many old houses, with fortified rooftops and no ground-floor doorways, gives a sense of how deeply pervasive the violence was. Fozzano is a prime example – its feud was the backdrop to Prosper Mérimée's 19th-century blockbuster *Colomba*.

The stunningly sited Campomoro

LE SARTENAIS

🗺 J6   ℹ 14 Cours Soeur Amélie, Sartène

Coastal wilderness is a rarity in the Mediterranean these days, but the southwest of Corsica has remained astonishingly untrammelled. Forced out by pirates and the collapse of the wine industry, its inhabitants gradually left the maquis a century or so ago to the ghosts of their prehistoric ancestors, whose tombs and standing stones are still strewn over the countryside.

1 Dolmen de Fontanaccia
Known to locals as "The Devil's Forge", this late megalithic burial chamber comprises six huge boulders topped by a slab. It is best viewed in the warm light of the setting sun.

2 Vallée de l'Ortolo
Overlooked by grey granite cliffs, this quiet and secluded valley just south of Sartène perfectly encapsulates the region's austere beauty. Visit the Domaine Saparale vineyard (p73) to savour the valley's vintage wines.

3 A Casa di Roccapina
🚗 RN196 📞 04957 15630 🕘 9am–4pm Tue–Sat ♿
This museum covers the history and legends of the region's bizarre *tafoni* rocks and humanmade shelters (*oriu*), and offers an audio-guided walk.

4 Musée Départemental de Préhistoire Corse et d'Archéologie
The finest collection of prehistoric artifacts on the island, some from the Neolithic age, are housed at this museum (p47). Among the items here, the obsidian arrowheads from Sardinia are worth a look. It is an ideal primer for tours of this region's standing stone sites.

> 🍴 **EAT**
> For lunch, drop into the roadside Bergerie d'Acciola (p93), which serves regional fare made with ewe's cheese.

here. More than 250 statue-menhirs cluster in this clearing.

7 Tizzano and Cala di l'Avena

Huddled around an inlet hemmed in by boulder-studded hills, Tizzano is among the island's most remote fishing villages.

8 Sartène

Sartène, described as "the most Corsican of Corsican towns" by author Merimée in the 19th century, is home to medieval buildings. The Easter U Catenacciu parade is notable.

9 Plage d'Erbaju

Clamber to the top of the headland overlooking Roccapina's white beach, crowned with a watchtower and rock outcrop resembling a recumbent lion, to pick up the path to a deserted beach (*p57*).

(*p57*)

10 Sentier des Douaniers

The former Genoese custom officers' path is now a world-class coast walk. It takes you along the Sartenais shoreline via a non-stop parade of wild beaches and coves.

Ancient burial ground, Dolmen de Fontanaccia

5 Site Archéologique de Cauria

This fascinating Neolithic site holds the Stantari and Rinaghju alignments, with 22 unique phallic menhirs amid the maquis south of Sartène.

6 Alignement de Palaggiu

The largest collection of standing-stones in Corsica can be found

Clockwise from left **Menhirs, Alignment de Palaggiu; artifact at Musée Départemental de Préhistoire Corse et d'Archéologie; lighthouse along Sentier de Douaniers; Sartène**

BONIFACIO

V K7 | 2 Rue Fred Scamaroni, Quartier Pisan; bonifacio.fr

Bonifacio is Corsica's foremost visitor attraction and, despite the overtourism in high season, it more than merits the distinction. Spread over the top of a long, narrow promontory that is encircled on three sides by sheer chalk escarpments with a vast citadel, the medieval Genoese *haute ville* (upper town) looks on one side across the straits to Sardinia and on the other over its secluded harbour.

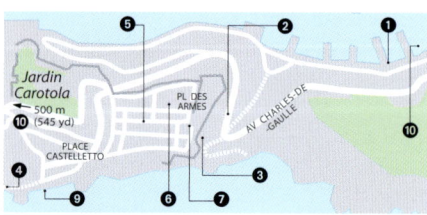

4 Escalier du Roi d'Aragon

⌂ Haute Ville, Bonifacio
◷ Apr–Sep: 9am–7:30pm daily (Jul & Aug: to 10:30pm daily); Oct: 10am–4:30pm daily ↗

Get hands-on experience of Bonifacio's chalk cliffs with a hike down this flight of 187 steps to reach a hidden well.

1 Quai Comparetti

Quai Comparetti's café-restaurants are the perfect place to soak up the atmosphere of Bonifacio's lively marina, with its boats and yachts.

2 Montée Rastello

This flight of stone steps leads from the port to a raised balcony below the entrance to the citadel, for a stunning view of the "Grain de Sable" rock stack and cliffs.

3 Chapelle Roch

This tiny shrine at the head of Montée Rastello is where Bonifacio's last plague victim died in 1518.

5 Ste-Marie-Majeure

Relics of the True Cross, said to have been donated by Emperor Constantine's mother, number among the treasures enshrined in Bonifacio's church.

Historic town of Bonifacio, with coastal views

THE WRECK OF THE SÉMILLANTE

They might look gorgeous on a sunny day, but the Straits of Bonifacio rank among the most fickle waterways in the world, with unpredictable currents. In 1885, the troop carrier *Sémillante* ran aground off the nearby Îles Lavezzi while en route to the Crimea. An obelisk on the westernmost islet commemorates the tragedy, in which 773 people lost their lives.

TOP TIP

Its customary to haggle when booking a boat trip.

6 Rue du Palais de Garde

Quaint multi-storeyed tenements with fine escucheon-embellished doorways flank this medieval street. Residents still use winches to lift supplies to upper floors.

7 Porte de Gênes

In Genoese times, this turreted gateway, with its impressive drawbridge, was the only entrance to the citadel. Beyond it

are breathtaking sea views from the Jardins des Vestiges.

8 Cimetière des Marins

At the western tip of Bonifacio lies a walled cemetery containing the decorated tombs of deceased Bonifacians.

9 Beaches Around Bonifacio

The chalky soils of the Bonifacio area helped create some of the Mediterranean's whitest, softest sand, especially in the nearby regions of Sperone, Pianterella and Rondinara.

10 Boat Trips
w spmbonifa cio.com

Hop on a boat to take a closer look at Bonifacio's resplendent white cliffs and *haute ville*. Some trips also take in the exquisite Îles Lavezzi off the coast.

Exploring the Cimetière des Marins

5

BASTIA

📍 F3 ℹ️ North end of Place St-Nicolas; bastia-tourisme.com

Bastia is Corsica's commercial capital, with a more upbeat , big-city feel than the city of Ajaccio. Since Genoese times, its nucleus has been a picturesque quarter of ramshackle old tenements, with buttressed walls and cobbled alleyways radiating from the harbour. The imposing twin bell towers of the 17th-century St-Jean-Baptiste church are the town's emblematic landmark. Behind the vibrant Vieux Port, an amphitheatre of high-rise suburbs look out to sea.

☕ **DRINK**
Le Coude à Coude (6 Rue du Dragon) is an ideal spot to savour a glass of Corsican red or to sample the island's unique white wines.

1 Musée de Bastia
📍 P6 📍 Place du Donjon, Citadelle ⏰ Hours vary, check website 🌐 musee.bastia.corsica

The Citadelle's fully renovated Governors' Palace holds a museum charting Bastia's evolution as a trade and artistic centre. Its collection includes part of Cardinal Fesch's hoard of Renaissance art (p25).

2 Cathédrale Ste-Marie and Oratoire Ste-Croix
This pair of majestic 15th-century Rococo churches in Bastia's Citadelle reputedly hold miracle-working icons: the former a silver Virgin; the latter a blackened oak crucifix, "Christ des Miracles", which was fished out of the sea in 1428.

Colourful buildings lining the marina, Bastia

3 Oratoire de l'Immaculée Conception
This Baroque chapel (1611) has an ornate interior. Behind the altar is a painting of the Immaculate Conception by artist Bartolomé Esteban Murillo.

4 Place St-Nicolas
Open to the sea on one side, Place St-Nicolas is where Bastiais come to wine, dine, stroll and play pétanque under the plane trees. A weekly flea market (open 6am–1pm) draws crowds on Sunday mornings.

5 Place du Marché
This square's name marché (market) derives from the stalls selling produce and local delicacies on weekend mornings here. There are also many cafés, perfect spots to people-watch.

Governors' Palace, home to the Musée de Bastia

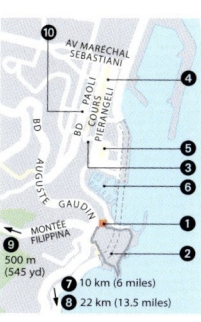

6 Vieux Port
Head to Bastia's old harbour at sunset, when the cafés around it cast reflections in the water.

7 DIAN' Arte Museum
🇫 F4 📍 5992 Lido de la Marana, Borgo 🕐 9am–noon & 2–6pm daily 🌐 gabriel-diana.com

This museum is dedicated to artist and sculptor Gabriel Diana (b 1942), who specializes in bronze

Bronze figurine at DIAN' Arte Museum

figures inspired by the Etruscan sculptures of his native Tuscany.

8 La Canonica
Dating back to 1119, the stately La Canonica (p49) is the finest of the 300 or so churches built by the Pisans across Corsica in the 12th century.

9 Scala Santa, Oratoire de Monserato
Bastia's most off-beat religious monument is a replica of the Holy Steps of St John Lateran's Basilica in Rome, which pilgrims ascend on their knees. Reach it from the Citadelle via the stepped Chemin des Fillipines.

10 Boulevard Paoli
Bastia's principal street is a grand thoroughfare, lined with impressive Napoleonic-era apartments and ritzy shops. The crowds usually begin to lessen after lunchtime.

BASTIA IN WORLD WAR II
Bastia witnessed the most intense battle fought on Corsican soil during World War II, when German officer Kesselring's army fled through the city. Due to a mix-up in the Allied command, a squadron of American B-25 bombers destroyed the Vieux Port as its inhabitants were out celebrating in the streets.

CAP CORSE

📍 E2 🚢 Port de Plaisance, Macinaggio; capcorse-tourisme.corsica

Before the construction of the corniche that circles Cap Corse in the 19th century, the long, finger-like promontory running north from Bastia was practically inaccessible except by sea. To a large extent, Cap Corse still feels like a separate island. The famous orange-blossom-scented muscat wine is still produced in the region by a handful of growers, whose terraces cling to steep, fire-blackened slopes.

are well worth the half-hour hike. Expect undulating cliffs and crashing waves.

2 Macinaggio
Located on the northeastern tip of Cap Corse, Macinaggio and its marina have a remote feel. To get much further north, you must go on foot or jump on a boat.

3 Tollare
A ribbon of tiny schist cottages clinging to the wave-lashed edge of Cap Corse, Tollare is the kind of place that makes you marvel at the resilience of its former inhabitants.

4 Nonza
Sweeping views across the Gulf of St-Florent extend from Nonza, a village atop a rock pinnacle, whose surrounding cliffs plunge to a beach.

5 The Corniche
The corniche winds around the entire cape. The section just north of Bastia has the best

1 Tour de Sénèque
The ancient Roman philosopher Seneca, exiled to a tower above the village of Luri, found the views from his prison over the northern cape "desolate", but they

DRINK
Sample the eponymous Cap Corse, a wine fortified with quinine (originally added as a malaria prophylaxis). Ask for "un Cap!"

Clockwise from top **Idyllic village of Nonza; sign at the entrance to a winery in idyllic Patrimonio; Genoese watchtower at the Site Naturelle de la Capandula; Centuri Port**

views, owing to its proximity to the Tuscan archipelago.

6 Conservatoire du Cap Corse de Canari

🌐 canarivillage.com
In the cellars of the former convent of St François, Canari has set up two permanent exhibitions. One is dedicated to traditional costumes, and the other to historic photographs taken on Cap Corse by 120 local families.

Hiking the Sentier des Douaniers trail

7 Erbalunga

A Genoese watchtower stands guard over Erbalunga's harbour, the prettiest port on the cape's eastern shore. Bastiais drive up here to dine at the fine Le Pirate restaurant *(p105)*.

8 Patrimonio

Some of Corsica's finest wines originate in the undulating terrain of Patrimonio *(p101)*, where white cliffs frame views of the bay. The 17th-century church of St Martin is worth a look.

9 Site Naturelle de la Capandula

A trio of idyllic beaches, backed by isolated Genoese watchtowers, provide the main incentive to follow the Sentier des Douaniers (old custom officers' path) to this nature reserve.

10 Centuri Port

Centuri's neatly painted fishers' houses, set around the tiny, quaint harbour, are truly picturesque. Its traditional seafood restaurants keep the lobster boats busy.

SAINT JULIE

One of Corsica's patron saints, Saint Julie was executed by the Romans in 439 CE for refusing to renounce her Christianity. Nonza's church of Saint Julie was built in her honour. A path leading down from the church to a black sand beach passes a sacred spring fountain, which is said to have sprung up after the saint's death. For centuries, pilgrims have believed its waters to have healing powers.

ST-FLORENT AND THE NEBBIO

📍 E3 🏛 Bâtiment Administratif, Rte Principale 53, 20217; corsica-saint florent.com

The Col de Teghime (Teghime Pass), separating Bastia from the Golfe de St-Florent, marks a shift in landscape, from the intensively cultivated east coast to the mountainous Nebbio region – Corsica's proverbial "Land of Mists". Press any further west and you venture into the Désert des Agriate.

1 The Quayside
St-Florent has a charming marina that entices a steady flow of sailing enthusiasts over from the French Riviera. Founded by the Romans, the town is also home to a striking mix of architectural styles with a number of sea-facing bars and pizzerias.

2 Citadelle
The bastion on the hillock above the harbour was built in 1439. It was bombarded by Horatio Nelson's fleet in 1794 and restored in 2000. The terrace has great views of the gulf.

3 Plage du Lotu
Le Popeye (lepopeye. com) offers a 20-minute boat cruise out across the gulf from Porte de St-Florent to the Plage du Lotu (p57), where turquoise shallows are patrolled by wild cows.

4 Plage de Saleccia
An hour-long hike from Lotu brings you to this wild beach (p56). Here, you can take a leisurely boat ride or enjoy a swim – but note that the water is known for tidal rips.

TOP TIP

For grocery shopping and souvenirs, stroll along Place Doria, which winds its way up to the Citadelle.

Relaxing on the white sands of Plage du Luto

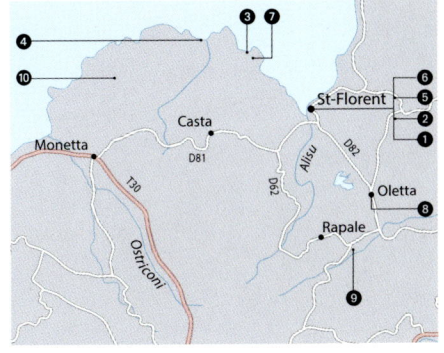

The charming quayside of St-Florent

5 Place des Portes

Pétanque, pastis and *passeggiata* – the "three Ps" – are the chief pastimes in St-Florent's main square, where a trio of terrace cafés compete for custom in nonchalant Corsican style.

6 Santa Maria Assumpta

Stroll up St-Florent's town square to reach the Pisan Church of Santa Maria Assumpta (p49). Inside its walls is a glass-sided coffin with the relics of St Flor, a Roman soldier.

7 Tour de Mortella

This watchtower (p53) inspired Admiral Nelson to build a string of lookalike "Martello Towers" along the coasts of Britain and Ireland.

8 Oletta

Oletta is a typical Nebbio village set high in the hills. Pisan sculpture embellishes the façade of the village's 18th-century Église St-André.

9 San Michele de Murato

Perched on a high terrace at the head of the Nebbio, this 12th-century chapel (p48) features chequered bands of green schist and yellow marble

10 Désert des Agriates

Hire mountain bikes from the small village of Casta to explore trails crisscrossing this moonscape of dried river beds, cacti and maquis-shrouded hills (p62).

NELSON IN CORSICA

A forgotten naval campaign in Corsica provided future admiral Horatio Nelson with valuable tactical lessons. Nelson was dispatched to the island in 1793 as part of Lord Hood's fleet to support Pascal Paoli's insurrection against the French. The attack at St-Florent went well enough, but the town of Calvi proved a much tougher nut to crack – costing Nelson the sight of one eye.

Romanesque façade of San Michele de Murato

CALVI

📍 B4 ℹ️ Port de Plaisance, 97 Chemin de la Plage; balagne-corsica.com

Calvi has been a seaside resort since the 1920s, when aristocrats from the Côte d'Azur came to pursue illicit affairs in clubs such as the legendary Chez Tao. Rising straight from the waves, Calvi's vast Citadelle is easily the most imposing of Genoa's former strongholds. In clear weather, the snow-streaked Corsican mountains seem so close you could almost touch them.

1 Quai Landry

Café-restaurants line the ritzy Quai Landry, Calvi's chic sea-facing quarter. It's the perfect place to buy a coffee or cocktail by the water and people-watch.

2 La Citadelle

📍 Quai Landry, Ville Haute 📞 04953 83393

Built in the 13th century, this stone fortress houses the St-Jean-Baptiste cathedral, the Tour du Sel (where salt tax was levied) and the Maison Colombe, a derelict cottage controversially claimed to be the birthplace of Columbus.

3 St-Jean-Baptiste

📍 Citadelle 📞 049 56 51667 🕐 8am–6pm

This grand 13th-century octagonal-domed cathedral is the focal point of Calvi's Citadelle. A crucifix that allegedly saw off the Turkish siege of 1553 is its prized possession.

> **TOP TIP**
>
> Take the U Trinighellu (p69) to reach one of the area's loveliest beaches, Plage de Bodri.

Narrow alley lined with shops in Calvi

4 Ste-Marie Majeure

🏠 Between Rue Clémenceau & Blvd Wilson, Ville Basse 📞 04956 50072 🕐 8am–6pm daily

The 17th-century belfry of St-Marie Majeure, built in the Baroque style, dominates the backstreets of Calvi's old town, where restaurant tables spill across terraces on a square on summer evenings. The city's fascinating Good Friday parade starts here.

5 Calvi Beach

Backed by a shady pine forest, Calvi's beach gently arcs in a picturesque curve of soft, pale-orange sand and crystal-clear turquoise water around the gulf's southern rim. It's the ideal spot for relaxing.

6 Calvi Marina

Some of the gleaming yachts in this marina have to be seen to be believed. The harbour pier affords splendid views of the waterfront and Citadelle.

7 Calenzana

At the start of the GR20 (*p62*) mountain trail, this village inland from Calvi centres on the Baroque Église St-Blaise, noted for its 17th-century tabernacle.

8 The Trinighellu

Calvi's single-carriage tramway train (*p69*), known as U Trinighellu (little train), rattles several times daily along the beautiful Balagne coast, heading as far as L'Île Rousse. It stops at a string of pretty beaches,

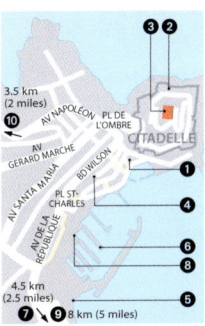

as well as at some of the island's off-the-beaten-track resorts.

9 Lumio

High up on the hillside, on the opposite side of the gulf from Calvi, is the picturesque village of Lumio, site of San Pietro, a Romanesque Pisan chapel founded in the 11th century.

10 Notre Dame de la Serra

The ultimate viewpoint over Calvi and its splendid gulf is the terrace of this atmospheric hilltop church. Readily accessible, it can be reached either in an hour's walk from the seafront or by car via a backroad off the D81.

The 15th-century Notre Dame de la Serra

CORTE

◙ D6 ⌂ La Citadelle; 04954 62670

With its 18th- and 19th-century buildings and spectacular mountain setting, Corte presents a very different aspect of the island from the Mediterranean chic prevailing on the coast. As the seat of Pascal Paoli's independent parliament, this was the crucible of Corsican nationalism. A strong sense of the island's cultural distinctiveness still pervades the streets here.

the ramparts of the Citadelle to reach this popular vantage point for panoramic views of the mountains.

4 Cours Paoli
Lined with slightly dilapidated yet charming buildings, Corte's main thoroughfare is a legacy of its pivotal role in the Paoli era. It is full of bars, restaurants and shops; the cafés at the south end are the liveliest during school term.

5 Citadelle
Perched on top of a near-vertical crag, the town's Citadelle is worth a visit for the views from over the crumbling *haute ville* (upper town) and mountains.

6 Oratoire St-Théophile
The Franciscan monk and freedom fighter Blaise de Signori, better known as St Theophilus, was the first and only Corsican to be canonized. He is honoured with this chapel sited close to his birthplace.

1 Treasure Hunt
Discover Corte's history and hidden architectural gems on a self-guided "treasure hunt" organized by the Altipiani agency. You'll need the help of locals to crack the clues.

2 Église de l'Annonciation
Joseph Bonaparte, Napoleon's elder brother, was christened in this mid-15th-century church on Place Gaffori. One of Corte's oldest buildings, this church houses a wax statue of St Theophilus, the town's much-loved patron saint.

3 The Belvedere
Clamber up a flight of stone steps beneath

EAT
Patisserie Casanova (*patisserie-casanova1887.fr*), on the corner of Cours Paoli and Avenue Xavier Luciani, sells freshly baked local specialities.

7 Place Gaffori
Walls still pock-marked by musket fire from the 1740s set the tone of this

Fountain in Corte's main thoroughfare, Cours Paoli

Corte's towering Citadelle atop a crag

picturesque square in Corte's *haute ville* (upper town). A statue of independence hero, General Gaffori, points stridently skywards.

8 Musée de la Corse

w museudiacorsica. corsica

Corte's cutting-edge museum showcases the island's traditional culture with fascinating exhibitions on farming, shepherding, religious brotherhoods, tourism and music. Your ticket also includes entry to the adjacent Citadelle.

9 Vallée de la Restonica

A narrow road from Corte runs to this beautiful valley. Jump on the shuttle bus in summer to reach Bergeries de Grotelle (shepherds' stone huts) and the lakes beyond.

10 Vallée du Tavignano

A wild, deep trench running from Corte to the fringes of the watershed, the Vallée du Tavignano shelters pine forests

A NATIONALIST STRONGHOLD

Corte occupies a prominent position in the hearts and minds of local nationalists. It was here that in 1755 Pascal Paoli convened his Assemblée Nationale, which founded the first Corsican-language printing press and drafted the Corsican constitution. Corte was also chosen as the site of the island's only university – a bastion of nationalism to this day.

and huge gorges. The area is accessed by walking a cobbled Genoese mule trail.

GOLFE DE PORTO

B6 | Porto Marina

The combination of red porphyry and lapis-blue sea have made the Golfe de Porto Corsica's defining landscape. No other place in the Mediterranean has such a striking juxtaposition, which is all the more astonishing for its backdrop of high mountains. Even at the height of summer, it is possible to avoid the crowds by taking to the network of paved mule trails through the gulf's forested hinterland, or heading for the area's lesser-known coves.

1 Girolata
The most picturesque village on the island, Girolata lies beneath the salmon-pink cliffs of Scandola. It can be reached on foot from Col de la Croix or by boat from Porto.

DRINK
Sip a chilled muscat on the lovely terrace of Les Roches Rouges *(p87)* in Piana in the after-noon, when the views are best.

2 Porto
Porto is an ideal base for trips around the bay and the perfect spot for a wide range of watersports.

3 Plage de Porto
Broad, steeply sloping and covered in dusty grey pebbles, this is not the most inspiring beach in the area, but its rugged appearance, complemented by the backdrop of dramatic cliffs, does make for a very scenic swim.

4 Porto's Watchtower
04952 61005
Apr–Oct: 9am–7pm daily
Dwarfed by the cliffs that surround it, this 16th-century watchtower offers fine views up the valley. A museum at the tower's base focuses on its history and the heather shrub.

5 Boat Trips
Several operators based in Porto offer boating trips to explore the area. In summer,

Bay of Girolata in the
Scandola Nature Reserve

7 The Corniche
This is Corsica's
model coastal drive,
but it can be a frustrating
stop-and-start expe-
rience in the summer.
Begin your journey in
the early morning, when
it's quiet, and the light
brings the red porphyry
to life.

**8 Plage de
Gradelle**
This secluded pebble
cove on the northern
shore of the Golfe de
Porto is reached via
a narrow backroad
off the main corniche.
The magnificent views
across the water are
its chief attraction.

9 Calanque Walks
The corniche
wriggles through
the rocks known as the
Calanques de Piana. To
see the views, follow one
of the trails outlined in
leaflets on sale at the
tourist offices in Porto
and Piana.

10 Capo d'Orto
The region's most
breathtaking viewpoint
(p86) is the domed sum-
mit of a vast sugar-loaf
mountain, Capo d'Orto,
whose north face looms
above Porto. A trail leads
you to the top and back
in around five hours.

**DRAGUT IN
GIROLATA**

Turgut Reis
(1485–1565), a
Greek-Ottoman
admiral and privateer
known as "Dragut",
was the scourge of the
Mediterranean in the
16th century. In 1540,
he and his fleet were
caught by the Genoese
in Girolata. He was in
captivity for four years
until his fellow corsair,
Barbarossa, forced his
release, whereupon he
promptly captured the
town of Bonifacio.
In 45 years at sea,
Dragut captured more
than 80 cities, towns
and islands.

---

excursion boats leave
daily for fishing trips
and tours of the gulf via
its rock formations, sea
caves and red cliffs.

6 Piana
With its white
houses, Baroque church
and the Calanques in
the background, Piana
occupies a prime posi-
tion overlooking the
Golfe de Porto. It is
the ideal base for
excursions along this
stretch of coastline.

Dramatic red rocks at Calanques de Piana

TOP 10 OF EVERYTHING

Fresh bread served at a local bakery

PREHISTORIC SITES

1 Filitosa
J4 **22 km (14 miles) N of Propriano** **Apr–Oct: 9am–sunset daily** **filitosa.fr**

This privately owned site in southwest Corsica has earned UNESCO World Heritage status for its statue-menhirs, many featuring skilfully carved faces and daggers – a trait of the island's Torréen population, who lived here nearly 4,000 years ago. There is a small museum on site.

2 U Nativu, Patrimonio
E3

In a shelter just south of Patrimonio church stands a superb statue-menhir known as "U Nativu", dating from 900–800 BCE. The statue bears distinct facial features and a T-shaped breastbone. Its face has become something of a mascot for this wine-producing area. In July, it is also given pride of place at the village's guitar festival.

Statue-menhir at U Nativu, Patrimonio

3 Alignement de Palaggiu
J6

Most of the 258 menhirs at this extraordinary site date from 1800 BCE. The grandfather of Corsican archaeology, Roger Grosjean, asserted that they must have functioned as some kind of deterrent to would-be invaders because of their proximity to the coast. To get to them, look for the turning just after the Mosconi vineyard on the left.

4 Pianu di Levie (Cucuruzzu)
A fairy-tale woodland of twisted oaks and mossy boulders enfolds the magical Pianu di Levie (*p89*) whose *pièce de résistance*, Cucuruzzu, is a well-preserved Torréen castle dating from around 1400 BCE – complete with living chambers and slab roofs. A second site, Capula, lies a 20-minute walk away.

5 Site Archéologique de Cauria
J6 **RD48 A**

Filitosa is more famous, but two of the menhirs at Stantari are the equal of their high-profile cousins in Valinco, with well-sculpted features, diagonal swords and sockets in their heads where horns must once have been. The Dolmen de Fontanaccia and Alignements de Palaggiu and Rinaghju are in the same area.

Collection of megalithic menhirs
at Filitosa

6 Musée Départemental de Préhistoire Corse et d'Archéologie, Sartène

📍 J6 🏠 Blvd Jacques Nicolaï, Sartène
📞 0495 77 0109 🕐 Hours vary, call
ahead 🗓 Public hols 💳

This collection of prehistoric artifacts
from all over Corsica is dominated by
Neolithic pottery fragments, obsidian
arrowheads and polished stone axes,
but also includes pieces of gold jewellery
and strings of coloured glass beads.

7 Dolmen de Fontanaccia

📍 J6

A granite structure dating from the
late megalithic period, when bodies,
previously interred in stone coffins,
were buried in stone chambers and
covered in compacted earth. Lost in
the depths of the Sartenais region,
this chamber ranks among the best
preserved in southern Europe. Its
former contents now reside in the
museum at Sartène.

8 Castellu d'Araggio

This amazing Torréen site (p92),
high in the hills north of Porto-Vecchio,
dates from 1500 BCE and has traces
of prehistoric cooking fires. The views
alone are worth a detour, and there is
a pleasant café, La Casette d'Araggio,
at the start of the path.

**Exploring the prehistoric fortress
ruins at Castellu d'Araggio**

9 The Pieve Menhirs

📍 E4

It is well worth making the trip to this
village in the hills overlooking St-Florent
to see its three statue-menhirs, which
stand together on a terrace of raised
ground next to the church. The family
group, chiselled some 3,500 years ago
from local granite, appear to be gazing
wistfully over the valley.

10 Musée de l'Alta Rocca, Levie

📍 K4 🏠 Ave Lieutenant de Peretti,
Quartier Prato, Levie 📞 0495 7 80073
🕐 Jun–Sep: 10am–6pm daily; Oct–
May: 10am–5pm Tue–Sat 💳

This museum in Levie has a single prize
exhibit: a human skeleton dating from
6570 BCE, known as "La Dame de
Bonifacio" (or "La Dame d'Araguina").
The woman died in her mid-30s and is
thought to have been disabled by
severely fractured legs.

CHURCHES AND CATHEDRALS

1 St-Jean-Baptiste, Bastia

📍 P5 🏠 4 Rue du Cardinal Viale Prelà, Place de l'Hôtel-de-Ville 📞 04955 52460 🕙 9am–noon & 3–6pm Mon–Sat

With twin belfries and a Neo-Classical façade, Corsica's largest church lends a typically Italian feel to the former Genoese harbour. The lavish rococo interior features gilt stucco, rare marble and a collection of trompe-l'oeil paintings.

2 San Michele de Murato

📍 E4

San Michele's trademark chequered pattern, rendered in grey green serpentine and off-white marble, entices a steady stream of admirers. Dating from the 12th century, the church preserves a wealth of reliefs of peculiar carved beasts and human figures – typical of the Pisan period. It is also one of the few medieval shrines still with its belfry.

Ornate Baroque Oratoire de l'Immaculée Conception

3 Oratoire de Monserato, Bastia

📍 F5 🏠 73 Chemin de Scala Santa 🕙 10am–6pm daily

Cleanse yourself of all sins as you ascend the Scala Santa in Bastia's famous Oratoire de Monserato. Only penitents able to make the pilgrimage on their knees may approach the altar at the top of the stairs, a privilege granted by the Pope.

4 Oratoire de l'Immaculée Conception, Bastia

📍 P5 🏠 Rue Napoléon 📞 04955 42040 🕙 9am–6pm daily

Dating from 1589, this church has witnessed innumerable civic events in its time, including the initiation of the island's colonial governors. It was also where the British Viceroy, Sir Gilbert Elliot, once presided over the island's parliament. The church's interior features velvet drapes and lashings of gold leaf. On the small square outside, black and white pebble-stones are laid out in the shape of a sun.

Pisan-style façade of Église de la Trinité et de San Giovanni

5 Église de la Trinité et de San Giovanni, Aregno
C4

This 12th-century Pisan masterpiece was built to look exactly like its contemporary, San Michele de Murato, in a chequered pattern of green and cream blocks. Rising from the edge of Aregno, this church is encrusted with wonderful allegorical carvings of mythical beasts and folk figures.

6 Santa Maria Assumpta, St-Florent
E3 **800 m (1 km) NE of Place des Portes** **Jun–Oct: 9:30am–noon & 3–6:30pm Mon–Sat**

Santa Maria Assumpta ranks alongside La Canonica as the finest surviving Pisan edifice on the island. With enigmatic carvings of writhing serpents and wild animals, its arched entrance reveals a Baroque interior housing the mummified remains of Roman centurion St Flor.

7 St-Martin, Patrimonio
E3

Now the symbol of the famous wine-growing region, St-Martin's bare, brown, schist campanile crowns the top of a wooded hillock and looks magnificent against the surrounding vineyards and chalk hills. Do not miss the famous

limestone statue-menhir "U Nativu" *(p46)* below it, which seems to be singing or howling.

8 La Canonica, near Bastia
F4 **Rte de la Canonica, Lucciana** **Jul–Aug: 9am–noon & 3–7pm daily**

Set on Bastia's southern fringes, this Romanesque cathedral was built in the early 12th century, on the site of a 4th-century basilica that was destroyed by successive invasions.

9 St-Jean-Baptiste, Calvi

Founded in the 13th century, Calvi's honey-coloured cathedral *(p39)* had to be rebuilt after the Turkish siege of 1553, when its principal statue – Christ des Miracles – was brandished from the ramparts to repel the attackers. The statue now enjoys pride of place in a chapel to the right of the choir.

10 Chapelle Ste-Christine, Cervione, Valle di Campoloro
F6 **2 km (1 mile) E of Cervione** **06163 57123**

This Romanesque chapel has twin apses nestled on a terrace overlooking the east coast near Cervione which retain late 15th-century frescoes. Its patron, Saint Christina, is depicted next to a kneeling monk. The chapel is signposted off the D71 and is only a short way from Cervione on the left.

VILLAGES

1 Evisa
Midway between the Golfe de Porto and Col de Vergio, the village of Evisa (*p85*) is swathed in chestnut forest. Paved mule paths dating from the Genoese era lead down pretty woodland walks to secluded swimming spots, and the local restaurants excel in traditional mountain cuisine.

2 Montemaggiore
C4
Montemaggiore straggles over a rocky ridge inland from Calvi, its ancient, buttress-walled tower houses huddled around a church tower that is dwarfed by the intimidating bulk of Monte Grosso behind. For the best views, climb the outcrop at the eastern entrance to the village, known locally as "A Cima".

3 Santa-Lucia-di-Mercurio
D6
The best reason to drive out to Santa-Lucia-di-Mercurio, on the south side of the Vallée du Tavignano (*p40*) in the Bozio region of central Corsica, is to admire it from a distance. Connoisseurs of great views will revel in the sight of its campanile and slate-roofed cottages set against the pale-grey crags and melting snow fields of distant Monte Rotondo.

4 Ste-Lucie de Tallano
K5
The orange-tiled rooftops of this Alta Rocca village, spread over a high balcony looking across the Rizzanese Valley to the Sartenais coast, are a magical sight from higher up the mountain. The village's 18th-century centre ranges around a square where you can have wood-baked pizzas next to a fountain.

5 Morosaglia
E5
This tiny village in the Castagniccia region is where Pascal Paoli was born, and where his ashes are enshrined in a marble-lined chapel. From its fringes, where a couple of Romanesque churches hide in the maquis, chestnut forest gives way to a panorama of high ridges.

6 Zonza
K4
One of the most clichéd images of the Corsican interior is that of Zonza, framed by the unmistakable Aiguilles

Village of Evisa overlooking the Forêt d'Aïtone

and cobbled lanes have not undergone much change since the time of the Savelli lords, who ruled from here in the 9th century.

10 Pigna

This thriving cobblestoned village *(p101)*, located in the Nervia valley, features houses that have been beautifully renovated into a chocolate-box vision with neat stonework and blue-painted doors and window shutters. Perched on a slope alongside olive orchards, the village has retained its medieval character, with stepped paths, narrow alleys and vaulted passageways. By the central square stands the local church with two bell towers. The village is known for its traditional Corsican music and arts and crafts.

de Bavella. This village, where Muhammed V, Sultan of Morocco, was exiled in 1952, lies a long trek from the granite peaks, but it is no less picturesque for all that, especially after a rare dusting of Mediterranean snow.

7 Ota

Before Porto's development as a tourist hub, Ota *(p85)* was the gulf area's principal village, and remains a far more charming spot. The rear terraces of its bars enjoy superb vistas across to Capo d'Orto's cliffs *(p86)*, while the Tra Mare e Monti Nord trail *(p63)* leads to some stunning viewpoints.

8 Tralonca

🗺 D6

Perched on the top of a conical hill on the opposite side of the valley from Corte, Tralonca lies about as far off the tourist trail as it is possible to get in Corsica. The village warrants a detour for its pretty core of square cottages, packed around a Baroque church amid miles of terraced fields.

9 Sant'Antonino

Situated at the summit of a conical hill in the Balagne region of northwest Corsica, the village of Sant'Antonino is the oldest inhabited settlement on the island. Its narrow vaulted alleyways

WATCHTOWERS AND LIGHTHOUSES

1 Tour d'Agnello
📍 E1

Atop a high promontory on the north coast of Cap Corse, this tower is a great vantage point over this wild and beautiful stretch of coast. Follow the path away from Barcaggio village for about 45 minutes, and try to visit in spring, when wild flowers carpet the surrounding clifftops.

2 Tour de Pinarellu
📍 L5

Rising from the crest of a low headland just north of Porto-Vecchio, this watchtower completes the perfect sweep of Pinarellu beach – a popular family hang-out in summer, where veterans of the infamous GR20 mountain trail come to ease their feet.

3 Tour de la Parata
📍 G3

The 12-m (39-ft) high Tour de la Parata dates from 1608. Its profile, rising from the top of a pyramidal headland at the northwestern tip of the Golfe d'Ajaccio, is echoed by that of the nearby Îles Sanguinaires (*p22*), receding like stepping stones out to sea. The views from the path leading to the end of the cape are stunning, especially at sunset.

4 Tour de Santa Maria, Cap Corse
📍 F1

This tower is one of 91 structures erected by the Genoese in the 15th and 16th centuries as an early warning system against pirates. Cleft in half, Santa Maria cuts a forlorn figure at the far end of a bay of blue water, surrounded by vineyards, maquis and rolling hills.

5 Tour de Capo Rosso
📍 A7

This spectacularly sited watchtower crowns a majestic red granite mountain at the southwest tip of the Golfe de Porto. Cliffs fall away to churning sea on three sides, while to the east a remarkable view unfolds over the bay to the high peaks inland. The trail starts 7 km (4 miles) west of Piana on the D824.

6 Phare de Pertusato
📍 K7

The most southerly spit of land in France, Capo Pertusato lies an hour's

The 19th-century lighthouse at Phare de Pertusato

9 Tour de Senetosa
H6

Put on your hiking shoes and trek a couple of hours through dense juniper scrub and myrtle bushes to reach the Tour de Senetosa. Built of white granite, it sits astride a rocky ridge next to a wind-powered lighthouse, overlooking a string of remote beaches. Pick up the path to it in Tizzano, and take along plenty of water.

10 Tour de Mortella, Désert des Agriate
E3

Nelson was so impressed with the Tour de Mortella when he attacked it in 1794 that he copied its design for a chain of structures along the southern shores of Britain – the so-called "Martello Towers". Visible from the excursion boats running to nearby Plage du Lotu, it can only be reached on foot via the coast path.

walk over the cliff tops from Bonifacio. Its lighthouse was constructed in 1838 to safeguard shipping in what still ranks among the most treacherous seaways in Europe. A stunning view over the Îles Lavezzi and Sardinia extends from the headland.

7 Tour de Capo di Muro
H4

Although less than an hour's drive from Ajaccio, Capo di Muro is as wild a promontory as any on the island. Locals wishing to get away from it all come here for a windy walk, heading down a rough path through the maquis to the tower crowning the headland's crest.

8 Tour de Campomoro
H5

The largest watchtower on the island, the 15-m (49-ft) Tour de Campomoro presides over a picture-perfect bay and contains Exposition Barbaresques an exhibition on the history of Corsica's watchtowers. Behind the tower lies a deserted shore, where bleached granite boulders have been eroded into extraordinary shapes. The path continues to Roccapina.

Admiring the Tour de la Parata from the nearby cliffs

NATURAL WONDERS

1 The White Cliffs of Bonifacio

◉ K7

Seagulls swarm above Bonifacio's corrugated chalk escarpments. The cliffs are so eroded at their base that they seem on the verge of collapse – which they have done in places, as shown by chunks of fallen debris. See them at their most striking on a boat trip out of the harbour.

2 Aiguilles de Bavella

A phalanx of seven mighty pinnacles soaring over a carpet of pine forest, the needle-shaped peaks of Bavella (p91) look like a vision from a fantasy novel. Whether viewed up close from the waymarked scrambling routes around their bases, or from the white Madonna statue at the Col, the needles present a truly breathtaking spectacle.

3 Laricio Pines, Forêt d'Aïtone

Some venerable old Laricio pines surviving in Forêt d'Aïtone (p84) reach a height of 50 m (164 ft), making them the tallest conifers in Europe. The Genoese used to prize the trees as ships' masts but they are now protected.

4 Scandola

Accessible only by sea, the terracotta headland at the northwest entrance to the Golfe de Porto is the most heavily protected land in France – a precious wild habitat and spectacular geological oddity. Experience the magical sea caves, giant osprey nests and porphyry rock formations around its fringes on a boat excursion out of Porto's marina.

White Madonna statue at the Col, Aiguilles de Bavella

the Niolo region. Natural pools in the river at its base offer plenty of swimming spots with views.

9 Bouches de Bonifacio
Divers queue near the waters of the Bouches de Bonifacio (p59) to visit a curious and tame colony of grouper fish. Slow-moving and faintly comical with their prominent lips, grouper (mérou) are the stars of the Corsican underwater world.

10 Calanche de Piana
▢ B7
The contorted orange granite of the Calanche de Piana covers the mountainside into the Golfe de Porto. The corniche cuts through the Calanche, giving access to a network of way-marked trails. While most are easily viewed from the road, some of the strangest rock formations can be seen on a boat trip from Porto.

Medieval town of Bonifacio perched atop limestone cliffs

5 L'Oriu de Canni
▢ K6
Shaped like a witch's hat, this rock (formerly a shepherd's shelter), rising above the tiny hamlet of Canni, is associated with all manner of spooky tales. Children will love its enigmatic appearance when the shadows lengthen in late afternoon.

6 Lac de Nino
Wild horses graze the green pastures surrounding this divine high-altitude lake (p98). A long, uphill walk is required to get here, but it is rewarded with the very first glimpse of the glass-like water, its surface reflecting the backdrop of snow-streaked peaks and ridges.

7 Paglia Orba
▢ C6
Soaring above the Vallée de Niolo, Paglia Orba, at 2,525 m (8,284 ft), is one of Corsica's highest mountains and a most distinctive peak, with a shark's-fin shape. The ascent – a 2-hour scramble from Ciottulu a i Mori refuge at its foot – is simpler than it looks from below.

8 Gorges de Spelunca
Towering cliffs flank this deep valley (p82), which snakes inland from Porto to the Col de Vergio pass into

BEACHES

Stunning crescent-shaped Plage de Santa Giulia

1 Plage de Santa Giulia
🗺 L6

If it weren't for the Corsican maquis and Mediterranean villas spread over the surrounding hills, this bay of dazzling aquamarine water and

soft white sand could be mistaken for the Caribbean. The beach gets jam-packed in the school holidays, as it lies within an easy drive of Porto-Vecchio and many of the island's campsites.

2 Plage de Saleccia
🗺 D3

The waters off Saleccia must be among the clearest in Corsica. Low rainfall in this desert area ensures minimal run-off from streams, leaving the shallows crystalline – perfect for snorkelling. The beach is as far-flung as it is beautiful. Camp in the site behind to enjoy seeing the sand turn red at sunrise and sunset.

3 Plage de Roccapina
🗺 J6

A lion-shaped rock formation and watchtower overlook water as transparent and sand as soft as anywhere in the Mediterranean. The beach is accessed via a badly rutted track, which often keeps the crowds at arm's length. Climb the path up the headland to the north for a bird's-eye view of this secluded cove.

4 Plage de Cupabia
🗺 H4

The sea at this glorious bay at the far northeastern end of the Golfe de Valinco can get choppy if there is a strong westerly wind. But in calm weather, the shallows are fine for kids to swim in. Facilities extend to a café, car park and basic campsite.

5 Plage de l'Ostriconi

Stroll along an easy path that crosses over a wooden bridge and through a little stream down to a gorgeous white and soft sandy bay. Families, campers from nearby campsites and an occasional herd of cows enjoy this quiet beach (p104). Note that there are no facilities here.

Strolling on the white sands of Plage de Rondinara

6 Plage de Rondinara
📍 L6

A clam-shaped lagoon entered via a slim gap between two headlands, this bay between Porto-Vecchio and Bonifacio does not attract the crowds you'd expect given how lovely it is – except in peak season, when the campsite behind it fills up. Bring your snorkelling kit – the underwater life is prolific.

7 Plage de Petit Sperone
📍 K7

This small beach is tucked away at the southeasternmost tip of the island, below a complex of millionaires' retreats and an exclusive golf course. You can reach the cove via a footpath from the beach at Piantarella nearby, where there is a rough lay-by to park in.

8 Plage d'Erbaju
📍 J6

Climb over the headland north of Roccapina and follow the track downhill to a spectacular 2-km (1-mile) sweep of coarse sand, with lots of space even at the height of summer. The chic Murtoli estate's rental cottages are the only buildings visible for miles.

9 Plage du Lotu
📍 E3

Catch a boat from St-Florent to reach this splendid beach with shining white sand and clear turquoise sea water, tucked away on the Désert des Agriate's pristine, rocky coast. The views across the gulf to the mountains of Cap Corse are unforgettable.

10 Plage de Palombaggia

Palombaggia's trio of gently shelving bays, lapped by shallow, turquoise water, are perfect for children. A row of stately umbrella pines provides shade in the dunes behind, and there is a terrific beach café at the southernmost cove – Tamaricciu *(p93)* – serving gourmet snacks and cocktails. During the summer months, jump on the bus to get here from Porto-Vecchio *(p89)*.

An outdoor café on the Plage de Palombaggia

Excursion boats moored at Girolata

BOAT TRIPS

1 Girolata and Réserve Naturelle de Scandola
🅿 A6

A fleet of excursion boats operated by Via Mare (*viamare-promenades.com*) chugs out of Porto's Marina during the summer from April to October, shuttling visitors out to the famous Réserve Naturelle de Scandola, with its soaring red cliffs. Boats stop for lunch at Girolata.

2 Golfe d'Ajaccio
🅿 H3

Ajaccio looks dazzling when viewed from the bay. Nave Va has boats (*naveva.com*) that leave Port Tino Rossi daily in summer for trips along the Rive Sud to Bonifacio, passing by Capo di Muro (*p86*). There is a stop for coffee and a swim en route.

3 Îles Cerbicale
🅿 L6

The highlight of boat trips offered by Chiocca Croisières (*amour-des-iles. com*) from Porto-Vecchio's harbour are the Îles Cerbicale, an archipelago of islets off Plage de Palombaggia (*p90*). Longer excursions continue on to Bonifacio and Îles Lavezzi, stopping for a dip at a secluded cove on the return leg.

4 Calanche de Piana

The sea caves and volcanic rocks of the Calanche (*p55*) feature on boat tours of the Golfe de Porto's southern shore. Porto Linea (*scandolagirolata. com*) offers boats that run from Porto as far as the foot of Capo Rosso, while full-day sailings cross the bay to Scandola and Girolata.

5 Sea Kayak Guided Tours

Cors'Aventure (*corse-aventure.com*) offers multiple-day sea kayak tours around Corsica's beautiful coasts from April to October, including tailor-made adventures. Some experience is necessary. Fees are all inclusive, covering high-quality equipment, meals and comfortable tents.

6 Cap Corse
🅿 F1

Jump aboard the charming San Paulu (*sanpaulu.fr*) in Macinaggio Marina or at Port de Plaisance for a jaunt along the beautiful north coast of Cap Corse (*p34*). The boat anchors for lunch at picturesque Barcaggio village. Trips also run to the nearby Italian island of Capraia.

Passing a beautiful rock arch in the Golfe de Porto

7 Îles Lavezzi
📍 L7

The Îles Lavezzi are a cluster of low-lying islets in the Straits of Bonifacio. Boats *(vedettesthalassa.com)* shuttle to and from them throughout the day, leaving you time to snorkel amid some of the Mediterranean's marine life.

8 Plage du Lotu
📍 E3

You'll never forget the first time you see beautiful Plage du Lotu *(p57)*. Take a rolling ride with *Le Popeye (lepopeye. com)* across the gulf from St-Florent, the cove's brilliant tur-quoise waters remain hidden until you are almost upon them. Depart early and you'll have plenty of time to enjoy a leisurely walk to Saleccia.

9 Santa Teresa di Gallura
📍 K7

The daily ferry ride by Moby Lines *(mobylines.com)* from Bonifacio to Santa Teresa di Gallura in the north of Sardinia is thrilling, affording superb views of the white cliffs of Bonifacio.

10 Golfe de Porto

Colombo Line *(colombo-line.com)* takes you from Calvi's Quai Landry *(p38)* around the northwest coast of the island to the Réserve Naturelle de Scandola and Calanche in the Golfe de Porto *(p42)*. The boats stop at Girolata for a scenic lunch overlooking the beach.

TOP 10 DIVE SITES

1. B-17, Calvi
📍 B4
Shot down in 1944, this American bomber rests in the turquoise water.

2. Les Cathédrales et les Aiguilles, Golfe de Valinco
📍 J5
These underwater mountain ranges are inhabited by 60 species of fish.

3. Le Tonneau and Red Canyon, Golfe de Valinco
📍 J5
There is exceptional diving on offer at these popular deep-water sites.

4. Capo di Muro, Ajaccio
📍 H4
The most southerly point in the gulf has abundant sea life.

5. Le Banc Provençal, Golfe de Lava
📍 G2
An Aladdin's Cave of rainbow wrasse and multicoloured sea sponges.

6. Vardiola and Punta Mucchilina, Golfe de Porto
📍 A6
Coral is abundant at these two sites.

7. L'Ila Morsetta, Galéria
📍 B5
This giant underwater boulder in Galéria choke teems with conger eels and lobster.

8. Mérouville, Bouches de Bonifacio
📍 K7
Large colonies of surprisingly tame grouper fish are the main draw of this celebrated dive site.

9. Pain de Sucre and la Canonnière, Bastia
📍 F3
The impressive rock formations of Pain de Sucre and la Canonnière lurk in the seas just north of Bastia.

10. Le Danger du Toro, Porto-Vecchio
📍 L5
Cliffs plunge to 40 m (131 ft) at Le Danger du Toro, where you can see abundant red coral reefs, large colonies of grouper and an impressive canyon.

OUTDOOR ACTIVITIES

1 Hiking
w pnr.corsica
Take to the network of long-distance hiking trails to explore Corsica's rugged interior. Ranging from two-day coastal ambles to the two-week marathon of the GR20 *(p62)*, the routes are all well equipped with hostels and huts.

2 Canyoning
w corse-montagne.com
This adventure sport, in which you climb and abseil through stream gorges using ropes and harnesses, has caught on fast in Corsica. The island's side valleys offer many possibilities for outfits running guided trips.

3 Via Ferrata
w viaferrata.org
Winding up spectacular rock faces and ridges, via ferratas enable climbers to navigate mountain routes without needing to use their own ropes.

4 Mountain Biking
The tracks winding through Corsica's magnificent forests and along the more open stretches of coast make for some superb rides. A very popular route is the 11-km (7-mile) cycle through the Désert des Agriate to Saleccia *(p36)*.

5 Snorkelling and Diving
w divingcorsica.com
Corsica's underwater topography is no less spectacular than the terrain on dry land, with sudden drops from sandy-bottomed bays to blue voids nearly 1,000 m (3,300 ft) deep in some places. Multicoloured fish are a common sight while snorkelling, and dive prospects rank among the most exciting in Europe.

6 Skydiving
w corseparachutisme.fr
Keen to experience the island's breathtaking mountainous topography from a completely unique perspective? Take the plunge and opt for skydiving. Corse Parachutisme is a popular dropzone in Propriano. Several diving schools on the island, including the Ecole de Parachutisme du Valinco in Propriano *(corseparachutisme.fr)*, offer tandem skydives, accelerated free-fall training and initiation jumps with trained and experienced guides.

Skiing off piste on the slopes of E'Capannelle

7 Skiing

W shiinfo.fr/corse/stations-de-shi

Corsica is not exactly known as a winter sports destination. However, if you happen to be on the island after a rare blizzard, join the exodus to the three surviving ski stations at Val d'Ese (northeast of Ajaccio), Vergio (Niolo) and E'Capannelle (Ghisoni), which all offer fine downhill runs.

8 Adventure Parks

Areas of forest across the island have been equipped with cable bridges, aerial walkways and zip slides to create assault courses. Get your pulse racing with these activities at Corsica Madness (p69).

9 Rock Climbing

W escalade-corse.com

Corsica has a number of rock-climbing hot spots. The most famous of them are the Aiguilles de Bavella in the south, the red escarpments crenelling Paglia Orba (p55) and the north face of Capo d'Orto (p86), near Porto.

10 Kayaking

W corsekayak.com

Beach-hop along the wilder stretches of Corsica's coastline by rented kayak. Organized expeditions involve bivouacs in deserted coves and circumnavigating promontories such as Scandola and Capo Rosso. Cors'Aventure offers private kayaking (p58) tours as well.

Mountain biking on a rocky path, Désert des Agriate

TOP 10
SCENIC VIEWS

1. Monte Cinto
📍 C6
On a clear day, you can see the distant Alps from Corsica's highest summit at 2,706 m (8,878 ft).

2. Monte Corona
📍 C5
See an astounding panorama from this mountaintop above Calenzana.

3. Notre-Dame-de-la-Serra
📍 B4
The views over the Golfe de Calvi from this hilltop chapel are magnificent.

4. Monte San Petrone
📍 E5
This peak offers views over the chestnut forests of Castagniccia (p97).

5. Capo Rosso
📍 A7
Climb this headland for a vista over the Calanche and gulf to Paglia Orba.

6. Chemin des Crêtes
📍 H3
There are superb views over the capital and its gulf from this high path.

7. Tour de Roccapina
📍 J6
This tower overlooks a paradise cove and a vast empty beach of white sand.

8. Capo Pertusato
📍 K7
The culmination of Bonifacio's white cliffs gives a view across to Sardinia.

9. Foca Alta, Cartalavonu
📍 K5
This high pass set in the Massif de l'Ospédale above Porto-Vecchio (p89) overlooks the southwest coast.

10. Capo d'Orto
📍 B7
This domed peak provides a great vantage point over the Golfe de Porto.

Notre-Dame-de-la-Serra views

Hiking the GR20, which traverses Corsica

TREKS AND WALKS

1 GR20
📍 C5

Corsica's legendary high-altitude trek, tackled by around 18,000 people each year, ranks among the most challenging multi-stage itineraries in Europe. This tough 11–15-day adventure is not to be undertaken lightly.

2 Evisa–Ota
📍 B7

This is a popular half-day walk through the fragrant chestnut forest that separates two of the island's prettiest hill villages. Tackle the paved Genoese mule track uphill from Ota or start in Evisa. Midway, the Pont de Zaglia spans a stream, and makes for a gorgeous picnic and swimming spot.

3 Mare a Mare Nord
📍 G1

A classic coast-to-coast route, this trail winds across the island at its widest point, via a parade of scenic highlights, including the Gorges du Tavignano and Vallée de Niolo (p95). This is among the lesser-visited long-distance paths.

4 Mare a Mare Sud
📍 J5

A five-day traverse of the far south of the island, this trail is punctuated by *gîtes d'étapes* (lodges) where you can unwind after each stage. Landscapes vary from oak forest to grassy uplands, with many swimming spots en route.

5 Campomoro–Roccapina
📍 H5

A terrific two-day coastal hike along the rugged shoreline of the Sartenais (p28), this route is peppered with beautiful coves and watchtowers. However, navigation can be tricky and there is very little shade or water along the route.

6 Sentier des Douaniers, Cap Corse
📍 F1

A two-day coastal itinerary around the wild northern tip of Cap Corse (p34), this trail takes in turquoise bays and scrubland. Starting at Macinaggio, it winds to Centuri Port, via an overnight stop at Barcaggio.

7 Sentier Littoral, Désert des Agriate
📍 D3

Three days are generally advised for this wild coastal hike along the edge of the Désert des Agriate. There is a campsite at Saleccia and a refuge at Plage de Guigno, but there are no other facilities. In early summer you'll have the stunning beaches all to yourself.

8 Tra Mare e Monti Nord
☑ B4

This is Corsica's second most popular walking route after the GR20 and takes you through the red-granite landscapes of the northwest. The pretty village of Girolata (*p58*), with its beaches and mountainous hinterland, is the route's highlight.

9 Lacs de Melo et Capitello
The path up the grandiose Restonica valley to this pair of exquisite glacial lakes (*p95*) gets jammed with hikers in high summer, but follow it in May or September and you are in for a treat. The ultimate reward is a vast amphitheatre of rock, scree and snow surrounding two shimmering blue lakes, formed at different altitudes.

10 Trou de la Bombe
☑ L4

This family-friendly amble takes you through the soaring granite pinnacles and pine forests of Bavella en route to the famous Trou – a large hole created by wind erosion in a vast escarpment. Climb up for dizzying views down to the coast.

Enjoying the view from the Trou de la Bombe

TOP 10 TREKKING TIPS

A mountain campsite

1. Wild Camping
It is illegal to wild camp in Corsica, so plan your accommodation in advance.

2. Booking Gîtes
Beds in lodges should always be booked well ahead. Full board is generally obligatory.

3. Refuges
Refuge places are allocated on a first-come-first-served basis.

4. Waymarks
Do not venture away from the waymarks unless you have the navigation skills to find them again.

5. Water
Always check with the locals about water sources, and take along a spare bottle in case you run out.

6. Sun
Underestimate the power of the Corsican sun at your peril. Sunstroke at high altitude can be lethal.

7. Guide Books
The Féderation Française de la Randonnée Pédestre (FFRP) publishes excellent guides for all Corsica's long-distance routes (*ffrandonnee.fr*).

8. Hygiene
Dispose of toilet paper responsibly; do not leave it on the trails.

9. Trekking Poles
Carry a pair of adjustable trekking poles to ease the knee strain on long ascents and descents.

10. Fuel
If you plan to cook, take a multi-fuel stove, as not all makes of gas canister are available in Corsica.

CORSICAN WILDLIFE

Bearded vulture (lammergeier) in flight

1 Bearded Vultures (Lammergeiers)

Europe's largest native birds of prey stand 1.2 m (4 ft) high, with wingspans up to 2.7 m (9 ft). They nest on rocky ledges in Corsica's highest valleys. Some 80 per cent of their diet is bone marrow, obtained by dropping bones from a height.

2 Corsican Deer

Based on the island for over 8,000 years, Corsican deer have evolved with shorter legs than other red deer. Although the last one was killed by a poacher in the 1960s, individuals of the same species have been successfully reintroduced from Sardinia into the Parc Naturel Régional de Corse.

3 Hermann's Tortoises

These tortoises with yellow-and-black-patterned shells live in the maquis, but have become endangered on Corsica as a consequence of wildfires and road accidents. Visitors are welcome to visit the Parc Naturel Régional's breeding centre at the Village des Tortues de Moltifao *(p68)*.

4 Corsican Nuthatch (Sitelle)

France's only endemic bird, the 12-cm (5-in) blue-grey, black and white sitelle inhabits Corsica's Laricio pine forests and lives primarily on a diet of pine nuts. It has the curious habit of walking down tree trunks headfirst.

5 Golden Eagles

High mountain dwellers, golden eagles have been clocked diving for their prey (usually hares) at 200 km/h (125 mph). Corsican shepherds used to chant magic spells on Christmas Eve to keep them away from their lambs. There are some 30 nesting pairs in the Parc Naturel Régional, with efforts to increase their numbers.

6 Wild Boar

One of the island's most common animals, boar often mate with wild pigs. They are quite shy, but if you meet a sow with piglets in the woods, you should walk quietly away to avoid disturbing their routines (and they can be aggressive when defending young).

7 Mouflons

Notable for their large, curling horns, Europe's only wild sheep were introduced to Corsica from Anatolia in Neolithic times. Now the island's emblematic animal, they gave their Corsican name to the polphonic

Mouflon, or wild mountain sheep

Corsican donkey grazing along the coast

musical group I Muvrini. Look for them leaping fearlessly over steep ledges in the Parc Naturel Régional.

8 Corsican Donkeys

Introduced to the island by the Romans, the Corsican donkey has long been a resilient companion to the island's inhabitants, performing the hard work of carrying goods and supplies across the island's steep terrain for centuries. It is now endangered, and there have been calls for it to be recognized as a separate species from other deer.

9 Corsican Fire Salamander

The island's native salamander owes its name to its bright yellow or orange markings. This fascinating creature thrives in moist environments, as it requires humidity to survive and breeds in fresh water. It is most often found in the deciduous mountain forests of the island, particularly at moderate altitudes, near freshwater streams or shaded ponds. You may find one hiding in a cool spot on a hot summer's day. In recent years, threats to the species have included habitat loss due to water pollution and wildfires.

10 Ospreys

The only large bird of prey to live exclusively off fish, the osprey is one of the great conservation success stories of the Réserve Naturelle de Scandola (*p54*). Reduced to only four nesting pairs in 1970, today around 30 of their messy seaweed-and-driftwood nests can be seen on the porphyry cliffs.

TOP 10 CORSICAN PLANTS

1. Laricio Pines
Corsica's majestic native pines have distinctive pyramidal crowns and grow as high as 50 m (164 ft); the oldest are in the Forêt d'Aïtone (*p54*).

2. Olive Trees
Introduced by the ancient Greeks, some trees in the Balagne are over 2,000 years old. Six varieties are made into Corsica's prized AOP olive oil.

3. Sweet Chestnut
Corsica's Castagniccia is the largest chestnut forest in Europe. The crop is made into flour and beer.

4. Fenouil
One of the strongest scents of the maquis comes from wild fennel, which is often used to flavour fish dishes.

5. Myrtle
This small tree is a symbol of love and immortality. Its dark-blue berries are used to make a liqueur.

6. Cistus (Rock Rose)
The Cistus blooms add a note of colour to the maquis between March and July.

7. Asphodel
Asphodel's long stalks and white flowers were traditionally associated with the dead and magic.

8. Arbutus (Strawberry Tree)
Bees make a prized honey from this maquis shrub's white flowers. Its berries are made into jam and liqueur.

9. Sweet Broom
In late spring and early summer, broom covers Corsica's hillsides.

10. Cork Oak
One of the few trees able to regenerate their bark, cork oaks grow mostly in southern Corsica.

Sweet broom in flower

WILD SWIMS

1 Plage de Guignu
D3 🏠 Refuge de Ghignu
📞 04955 91735 🕐 May–mid-Oct

A five- to six-hour walk from the nearest road on the Désert des Agriate coastal path brings you to this magical cove. Its turquoise waters lie beyond the reach of all but the most determined trekkers. The Refuge de Ghignu (The Paillers) provides basic lodging.

2 Cala Genovese and Cala Francese
F1

This pair of isolated coves is the jewel of Cap Corse's northern shoreline. Piles of seaweed sometimes mask their soft white sand, but the water is clear and the shallows are ideal for kids of all ages – though you'll probably have to carry young children most of the way from Macinaggio (p34).

3 Cascade des Anglais
In the early 20th century, these beautiful waterfalls (p98), high on the watershed near the railway station in Vizzavona, used to attract daytripping English aristocrats from Ajaccio – hence their name.

Now they are firmly on the tourist trail, thanks to the pine forest and grandiose mountain scenery on all sides. Call in for a coffee at the delightfully old-fashioned Hotel Monte d'Oro.

4 Plage d'Argent
J6

Appreciate the silver sand and turquoise water of the Sartenais coast in solitude at this remote cove. It can be reached after a 30-minute drive down a rutted track, opposite the turning for the Palaggiu menhirs (p29), followed by another 30-minute trek over the gravelly sand of Plage de Tralicetu.

5 Piscines Naturelles d'Aïtone
C6

This classic picnic spot is nestled under vast Laricio pine trees just below the Col de Vergio (p84). The roar of the falls is just as invigorating as the deep pools they flow into, and there are river-smoothed granite boulders to sprawl on after taking a relaxing dip.

6 Cala di Tuara
A6

After an hour's hot hike through the maquis dividing Girolata from the Col de la Croix (p86), Cala di Tuara is a welcome sight. Few can resist the lure of its amazingly clear water, shimmering blue above a bed of grey granite pebbles. The cove slopes down quickly and offers some terrific deep-water snorkelling.

7 Pont de Muricciolu, Albertacce
C6

This heavenly bathing spot high in the Vallée de Niolo, beside another

Splashing in the waters of the Cascade des Anglais

secluded old Genoese bridge *(p98)*, is generally the exclusive preserve of hikers following the Mare a Mare Nord path *(p62)*. You can walk to it in about 20 minutes from the D84 – look for the trail peeling north just after the crucifix on the outskirts of Albertacce village.

8 Lonca
☑ B6

Although a bit crowded at the height of summer, this popular bathing place in the secluded Lonca Valley deserves a detour from the nearby D124. Deep-green pools froth with water surging over granite slabs, shaded beneath a canopy of Mediterranean oak and chestnut forest. The site lies an easy five-minute walk from the road.

9 Pont Génois, Asco
☑ D5

A humpbacked, 16th-century Genoese bridge spans the stretch where the normally turbulent Asco river flows calm and deep. Bring a snorkel mask to see the trout that lurk in the river's green depths, and put on a pair of hiking shoes so you can explore the ancient path continuing up the mountain. Asco village lies 22 km (14 miles) west of Ponte Leccia on the D147.

10 Tuarelli
☑ B5

On the edge of this far-flung hamlet in Corsica's rugged northwest, the

Genoese Pont de Muricciolu in Albertacce

Fango river drains through smoothed boulders that shelter perfect natural pools to swim in when water levels are low during the summer. A huge wall of blood-red mountains – the "Grande Barrière" of Paglia Orba's north face – forms an enthralling backdrop as you splash about.

FAMILY ATTRACTIONS

1 Capo Pertusato Trail
📍 K7

Just before you reach the Capo Pertusato lighthouse *(p52)*, a short, dirt footpath leads down through dry maquis, weaving past wind-sculpted limestone rocks to a little sandy beach.

2 Village des Tortues de Moltifao

📍 D5 🏠 Route d'Asco, Tizzarella 🕐 9am–5pm Mon–Fri 🌐 village destortues.wordpress.com ↗

With Corsican tortoises becoming increasingly rare due to habitat destruction, the focus in this sanctuary, run by the National Park Authority, is on breeding endemic species for release into the wild.

3 Corsica Forest

📍 L3 🏠 On the D268 near Solenzara 🕐 Apr–Oct: 9am–6pm daily 🌐 corsica-forest.com ↗

Just inland from Solenzara, Corsica Forest has a very well-equipped adventure park and a challenging via ferrata facility around a massive cliff overlooking a bend in the river. Canyoning is an optional add-on.

4 Jardin des Abeilles

J3 ◗ Ocana, off D3 ◗ 9am–7pm Mon–Fri, 10am–7pm Sat & Sun lejardindesabeilles.com

Corsican honey is out of this world – especially the variety made from maquis or chestnut-flower pollen. Tours of this little bee garden just outside Ajaccio introduces the honey-making process.

5 Plage de la Tonnara

K7

Head to this easily accessible pink-sand beach just outside of Bonifacio for a picnic. Children can build sand castles and wade out into the lagoon-like crystal clear sea to spot colourful fish. Trails criss-crossing the area are great for family strolls. There are also several seafood restaurants here.

6 A Tyroliana

L4 ◗ Route de Taglio Rosso ◗ Apr–Oct: 10am–7pm daily atyroliana.com

A short drive inland from the coast around Porto-Vecchio, this riverside adventure park offers mountain biking, electric scooter rides and a mix of vertigo-inducing thrills in a shady pine forest, with pleasant picnic spots and river swimming nearby.

7 Tri-yaking

Rent a tri-yak – like a kayak, but with places for two adults and a child – for a paddle around the Pinarello bay and its adjacent island – ideal for beginners of sea kayaking. Sporsica (en.sporsica.fr), which operates from May to October, also offers quatro kayaks that seat two adults and two children, and pedalos – both are perfect for families to cruise around in.

Canyoning in the deep pools of Corsica Forest

Tramway de Balagne trundling along the Corsican coast

8 Tramway de Balagne

C4 train-corse.com

The train line across the mountains is one of the great experiences Corsica has to offer, but the journey can be a little too long for children. An option is to take the tramway train between L'Île Rousse and Calvi, also known as U Trinighellu, which skirts some fine beaches, stopping at 16 stations.

9 Corsica Madness

L4 ◗ Zonza ◗ May–Sep: 8:30am–8pm daily corsicamadness.fr

This sprawling adventure park, in a Laricio pine forest just below the Aiguilles de Bavella, occupies a most spectacular site with mountain views. Choose between canyoning, hiking and tours of an organic farm – exciting activities for all ages.

10 Parc Naturel d'Olva

J5 ◗ Route de la Castagna, Sartène ◗ Hours vary, chech website parc-animalier-corse.com

Children can mingle with a menagerie of free-roaming donkeys, goats, ponies, ducks, chickens and peacocks at this smallholding in the Rizzanese Valley, just below Sartène. There's also a café and a picnic area in the park.

LOCAL DISHES

1 Miel de Châtaigne (Chestnut Flower Honey)

If you like your honey strong and packed with flavour, pick up a pot of *miel de châtaigne* at a local deli and prepare yourself for a taste of heaven. Chestnut-flour biscuits provide the ideal accompaniment.

2 Tianu (Game Stew)

Corsicans are passionate hunters and will shoot anything that flutters in the maquis. Most of the small game ends up in hearty *tianu* (stew), typically made with *bécasse* (woodcock), *pédrix* (partridge), *caille* (quail) and other such birds.

3 Charcuterie

The diet of Corsica's free-range pigs – windfallen chestnuts, roots and wild berries – is the secret behind the island's aromatic cured meats. They come in a variety of forms: *prisutu* (ham); *lonzu* (fillet); *figatellu* (strong liver sausage); *coppa* (shoulder); *valetta* (cheek) and *salamu* (spicy salami).

4 Veal and Olives

This classic Corsican dish features on the menus of most Corsican restaurants all year round. Like the pigs, local calves tend to be grazed in the maquis, where they feed on unfertilized woodland and mountain pastures . The local veal is known for having a fuller flavour, which is perfectly complemented by the strong Alta Rocca olives used in this recipe.

5 Sanglier (Wild Boar)

Despite the annual onslaught from hunters in the winter, wild boar remain prolific in the forests of the Corsican interior. If you're here during hunting season, you'll find local menus dominated by wild-pork stews and fillets, grilled with maquis herbs in smoky open hearths

6 Pietra Beer

Corsicans have always dried chestnuts to make flour, and in 1996 local couple Armelle and Dominique Sialelli found that it also made a superb amber beer. One of Corsica's economic success stories, the brewery in Furiani produces a variety of beers and Corsica-Cola.

7 Chestnuts

The humble chestnut was once the staple food on the island when the Genoese planted whole forests of chestnut trees here. The flour derived from the dried nuts is still an essential ingredient in many traditional dishes and is widely used, particularly those of the mountains. Most patisseries in Corsica serve a wide range of cakes, pastries and bread made with chestnut flour.

Traditional charcuterie and delicatessen items

Crispy *beignets* served with ham, salami and goat's cheese

8 Beignets (Fritters)
Light and nutty, chestnut-flour *beignets* are a perennial Corsican favourite, often served as a starter. The best are made with *brocciu*. *Beignets* are often wrongly translated on menus as "doughnuts", which does not do them justice.

9 Fromage de Brébis (Ewe's Cheese)
Pungent and filled with mountain flavours, Corsican matured ewe's cheese derives its intensity from the herb-filled pastures the sheep graze on during the summer, and the cheese-making techniques used by shepherds, which have altered little over the ages.

10 Brocciu
Brocciu (pronounced "broodge") is soft ewe's cheese, produced uniquely in the winter. Corsicans love the full flavour and creamy texture it lends to many dishes. It blends wonderfully with mint for the filling in cannelloni and the stuffing for Bonifacio's traditional baked aubergine.

Corsican goat's cheese, *brocciu*

TOP 10 DRINKS AND APERITIFS

1. Ajaccio Blanc
The island of Corsica might be better known for its bold and robust red wines, but this refreshing, crisp white wine is certainly worth trying.

2. Nielluccio
Nielluccio is a prominent red wine grape variety that is widely cultivated across the island.

3. Cap Corse Muscat
These muscats are made from the renowned Muscat Blanc, à Petits Grains grape, regarded as one of the finest Muscat grapes in the world.

4. Chestnut Liqueur
This rich and warming drink has been made on the island for centuries. The smooth and aromatic liqueur captures the nutty essence of its star ingredients.

5. Pietra
Corsica's signature lager is easy to drink and incredibly refreshing, making it the perfect choice to quench your thirst after a rugged mountain hike.

6. Myrtle Liqueur
Myrtle liqueur, a fragrant spirit, is made from the berries and leaves of the myrtle plant, which grows abundantly in the wild landscapes of Sardinia and Corsica.

7. Cap Corse Mattei
The island's legendary aperitif, Cap Corse Mattei, is a refined and elegant fortified wine. It has a delicate balance of herbal and citrus notes and provides a refreshing flavour profile.

8. Fig Liqueur
Corsican fig liqueur is sweet and fragrant, and is carefully distilled from ripe fruits.

9. Mouss'or
A unique and flavourful local soda, mouss'or tastes like a delightful mix of apple and cinnamon.

10. Colomba
This excellent white beer has notes of several local herbs.

Domaine Pieretti vineyards, bordering the sea

WINERIES

1 Domaine Pieretti
📍 E2 🏠 Santa Severa, Luri, Cap Corse 📞 04953 50103 🕐 Apr–Oct: 10am–noon & 3–7pm Mon–Sat

Lina Venturi-Pieretti became the family's fifth-generation wine-maker in the late 1980s. The wines now produced owe their uniqueness to the unusual mix of Alicante and Niellucciu grapes, which thrive in the cape's dry, windy climate. Look out for the award-winning orange-scented muscat.

2 Domaine Leccia
📍 E3 🏠 Poggio d'Oletta, Morta-Piana, near St-Florent 🕐 9am–7pm Mon–Sat, 10am–6pm Sun 🌐 domaine-leccia.com

Corsican grape varieties Niellucciu (for reds) and Verminto (for whites) combine beautifully with the *terroir* of this third-generation vineyard in the

hills outside St-Florent. State-of-the-art production complement a traditional growing style to produce award-winning vintages.

3 Domaine Fiumicicoli
📍 J5 🏠 Rte de Levie, Sartène 🕐 Apr–Oct: 9:30am–2:30pm & 2:30–6:30pm Mon–Fri 🌐 domaine-fiumi cicoli.com

Aged in American oak barrels, the red cuvée, Vassilia, is the flagship wine, but of equal pride are the herb-tinged white and red muscat dessert wines.

4 Clos d'Alzeto
📍 H2 🏠 Sari d'Orcino, near Ajaccio 🕐 Winter: 9am–noon & 2–6pm Mon–Sat; summer: 8am–12:30pm & 1:30–6:30pm Mon–Fri, 9am–6:30pm Sat 🌐 closdalzeto.com

In a setting 500 m (1,640 ft) above sea level, Corsica's highest vineyards have been tended by the Albertini family since 1800. The unique microclimate yields fine, original wines: a spicy Sciaccurellu red, a clean, fruity Vermentinu and an exceptional rosé.

5 Domaine Gentile
📍 E3 🏠 Olzo, near St-Florent 🌐 domaine-gentile.com

Classic Corsican wines, including one of the island's top muscats, are produced by hand according to strict organic principles in this region.

Barrels of wine at the Domaine Leccia

The well-drained chalk-schist soil and sunny climate are perfect for wine-making, and the wines themselves are magnificent.

6 Domaine Antoine Arena
E3 **Morta Maio, D81, Patrimonio** **04953 70827**

Known as a "godfather" of Corsican wine, Arena produces a wine that is truly sublime – an expression of Corsican viticulture, identity and family values. Handed down for generations, the growing techniques have not changed over the years, and neither have the wines. It is advisable to book your visit in advance.

7 Clos Nicrosi
E1 **Rogliano, Macinaggio, Cap Corse** **May–Sep: 10am–noon, 4–7pm Mon–Sat** **vinsdecorse.com**

Founded in 1859, this lovely 25-acre (10-ha) vineyard nestled in the northern Cap Corse retains a distinctly Genoese overtone. The characterful wines it produces are much sought-after, but notoriously difficult to find unless you travel to the village of Macinaggio yourself. Its exceptional white and aromatic muscat varieties have cultivated a loyal following among local wine lovers. From November to April, the vineyard can be visited only by appointment.

8 Domaine de Torraccia
L5 **Lecci, near Porto-Vecchio** **Jan–Jun & Sep–Dec: 8am–noon, 2–6pm Mon–Sat; Jul & Aug: 8am–7pm Mon–Sat** **domaine-de-torraccia.com**

Christian Imbert was among the first to recognize the potential of Corsica's traditional vine stock and unique granitic soil in the 1960s. Grown organically, these hand-harvested grapes produce wines of remarkable distinction. Pick up a bottle of the vineyard's signature "Oriu", which is considered one of Corsica's finest reds.

9 Clos Culombu
B4 **Chemin San Pedru, Lumio, near Calvi** **May–Oct: 9am–7pm Mon–Sat, 10am–1pm & 3–7pm Sun; Nov–Apr: 9am–noon & 1:30–6pm Mon–Sat** **closculombu.fr**

On the outskirts of Lumio (p39), Etienne Suzzoni's organic vineyards tend towards quality over quantity. The aromatic wines have a strong Corsican character. Enjoy the pink-grey rosé with local snapper; the red comes oaked as "Clos Cuvée" or the more traditional "Domaine".

10 Domaine Saparale
J5 **Vallée de l'Ortolo, Saparale Sartène** **saparale.com**

Saparale is buried deep in one of the wildest corners of the Sartenais. You can taste the crisp minerals of the Vallée de l'Ortolo in Philippe Farinelli's light-bodied wines. Their rosé garners rave reviews.

FESTIVALS

Procession during La Granitola in Calvi

1 La Granitola, Calvi
Good Fri

Calvi's Easter begins at 9pm on Good Friday, when penitents carry wooden crosses through the *basse ville* (lower town) from the cathedral square.

2 La Cerca, Erbalunga
Good Fri

This Easter procession by masked brotherhoods begins at the church of St-Erasme on the outskirts of Erbalunga in Cap Corse.

3 U Catenacciu, Sartène
Good Fri

This procession of penitents draws its participants from *confraternità* (religious brotherhoods). Secrecy surrounds the identity of the red-robed Pénitent Rouge – a role often taken by repentant mafia godfathers.

4 BD à Bastia
Late Mar/early Apr W una-volta.com

The heart of Bastia's cartoon festival is an exhibition featuring an array of modern graphic art books, from time-honoured favourites such as Tintin to Marvel and anime.

5 Procession du Christ Noir, Bastia
3 May

The streets of Bastia's Citadelle form the backdrop for this religious procession, in which a black crucifix is paraded on the shoulders of devotees. The cross was discovered floating in the sea in 1428.

6 Rencontres Internationales de Théâtre en Corse, Olmi-Cappella, Pioggiola
Mid-Jul–mid-Aug W ariacorse.net

This village in the Giunssani region transforms into the venue for a drama festival. Villagers perform plays on open-air stages, and internationally famous directors help the participants prepare.

7 Festival du Film de Lama
Late Jul/early Aug W festilama.org

This niche film festival attracts film professionals from across Europe and features movies inspired by rural themes. Screenings take place in an

Re-enactors dressed as Napoleonic soldiers, Fêtes Napoléoniennes

open-air cinema on the outskirts of Lama (*p104*), where bourgeois houses stand in striking contrast to the surrounding barren mountain slopes.

8 Fêtes Napoléoniennes, Ajaccio

Mid-Aug ⓦ ajaccio.fr

Marching soldiers in First Empire uniform and sound-and-light extravaganzas bring a splash of pageantry to the Corsican capital in August, when the town celebrates the birthday of its most illustrious son. The grand finale, featuring an ear-splitting display of fireworks, is on Ascension Day (15 Aug).

9 Fête de l'Assomption de la Vierge Marie, Bastia

15 Aug

Marking the passage of the Virgin Mary, a street procession takes place in Bastia and other cities and towns throughout Corsica. The day ends with fireworks.

10 A Santa di u Niolu

Sep

This age-old festival sees the bars in the mountain village of Casamaccioli overflow with aficionados of a dying Corsican art form – *chama i rispondi*. The performers improvise insults in rhyming couplets.

TOP 10 COUNTRY FAIRS

1. Les Agrumes en Fête, Bastelicaccia
Feb ⓦ fetedesagrumes.com
Exhibitors display citrus produce at this fair. Some recipes even date from the court of Louis XV.

2. Festa di l'Oliu Novu, Sainte Lucie de Tallano
Apr ⓦ tallano.fr
Corsicans welcome spring by celebrating their hearty olive oil.

3. A Fiera di u Casgiu, Venaco
May ⓦ fromages-corse.org
The smell of delicious cheese permeates the air at the island's largest cheese festival.

4. Pescadori in Festa, Ajaccio
Early Jun
Fishers (and flavourful seafood) are the focus of two days of feasting and activities.

5. Fiera di u Vinu, Luri
Jul ⓦ fieradiuvinu.corsica
Sample Corsica's finest wines in an inspiring setting on Cap Corse.

6. Fiera di l'Avilu, Montegrosso
Jul
This fair in the Balagne mountains is dedicated to Corsican olive production and welcomes visitors from all over the world, passionate about the fruit and its virtues.

7. Fiera di l'Amandulu
Aug
A fair to promote Corsica's ailing almond industry.

8. Festa di u Ficu, Peri
Sep ⓦ festadiuficu.com
A long-standing celebration of the regions' fig production and local specialities.

9. U Mele in Festa, Murzu
Late Sep ⓦ u-mele-in-festa.com
Murzu, north of Ajaccio, celebrates honey from the maquis with a fair.

10. Fiera di a Castagna, Bocognano
Dec ⓦ fieradiacastagna.com
Food producers from all over the island present chestnut products.

Jazz performance during the Jazz in Ajaccio festival

MUSIC FESTIVALS

1 Jazz in Ajaccio
Late Jun W jazzinajacciu.com
This annual festival brings together big-name artists for a performance under the stars. It headlines everything from jazz and blues to modern and instrumental music.

2 Calvi on the Rocks
Mid-Jun/early Jul W calvionthe rochs.com
While not a big festival by international standards, this is great fun nonetheless. It is held at the height of summer, and bands and DJs play rock and dance music on open-air stages behind the beach.

3 Les Nuits de la Guitare, Patrimonio
Jul W festival-guitare-patri monio.com
This guitar festival, held in the square below the village's church, has seen an impressive line-up of stars. Both local and international musicians have taken to the stage here, including Murray Head (from "One Night in Bangkok" fame), The Stranglers and The Beach Boys.

4 Festivoce, Balagne
Mid-Jul W voce.corsica
Corsican vocal music forms the basis of this lively festival in Balagne. The larger events are staged in Pigna's modern, Moorish-style theatre. Free sunset serenades take place every evening of the festival.

5 Porto Latino, St-Florent
Aug W portolatino.fr
For four nights, St-Florent's Place des Portes resounds to salsa, mambo and Brazilian cumbia, as top-draw Latin dance groups take to the stage in this vibrant music festival.

Eddy de Pretto performing at Calvi on the Rocks Festival

6 Festival de Musique d'Erbalunga

Aug

A floodlit Genoese watchtower at the entrance to Erbalunga's tiny harbour provides a backdrop for this high-season festival, held in the village's little square. French jazz and "le Rock" dominate proceedings over the long weekend in the month of August.

7 Ballà Boum Festival, Patrimonio

Late Aug ⓦballaboum.com

Both local and international DJs spin techno, disco and house music for a two-day outdoor dance party held in Patrimonio's amphitheatre. Revellers can also indulge in an array of local street food and drinks.

8 U Settembrinu, Tavagna

Late Aug ⓦtavagna.com

This week-long event makes the most of the last days of summer – the local squares in Tavagna are transformed into lively open-air stages. Rock, world music and folk are its mainstay with a strong showing from Corsican polyphony fusion artists.

9 Rencontres de Chants Polyphoniques, Calvi and Bastia

Mid-Sep ⓦrencontrespolyphoniques.com

Corsica's most famous polyphonic choir, A Filetta, presides over this annual festival, which attracts artists from all over the world. Mongolian throat singers, Bulgarian women's choirs and Georgian monks have all appeared in the past.

10 Les Musicales de Bastia

Nov ⓦmusicalesdebastia.com

Mostly French and Italian stars perform at Corsica's oldest and last big music festival of the year. Performances take place over five nights at different venues in Bastia, ranging from the Second Empire theatre to the Oratoire Ste-Croix.

TOP 10 POLYPHONY ALBUMS

I Muvrini on stage

1. *A Bercy*, **I Muvrini**
This is a platinum-selling album of I Muvrini's performance at Bercy, Paris.

2. *Per Agata*, **Donnisulana**
An all-women ensemble's debut album, which took the Corsican music world by storm.

3. *Corsica Sacra*, **Jacky Micaelli**
One of the finest voices of her generation, Jacky was most expressive in this passionate recording.

4. *Intantu*, **A Filetta**
This group is renowned for its traditional and contemporary polyphony.

5. *A Cappella*, **Tavagna**
An old-school quintet from the island's eastern interior singing sublime polyphony.

6. *Polyphonies*, **Voce di Corsica**
A "supergroup" of Corsican singers formed in the 1990s. This album of polyphony ranks as among the island's most popular.

7. *L'Âme Corse*, **Various Artists**
An album showcasing Corsica's polyphony output, with some instrumental tracks.

8. *U Cantu di e Donne*, **Isulatine**
A mixture of original compositions by an all-women group.

9. *Isulanima*, **Trio Soledonna**
Traditional musicians from around the Mediterranean team up with three of Corsica's finest singers.

10. *Le Chœur de Sartène*
Traditional polyphony performed by the legend Jean-Paul Poletti and his male-voice choir group.

AREA BY AREA

Ghisoni, high in the mountainous interior

AJACCIO AND THE WEST COAST

Ajaccio, Corsica's flamboyant capital, has two distinct sections: the imperial city, with its pastel-washed alleyways and fishing harbour, and the suburbs of tower blocks spilling over the hills. Few visitors stray further from the waterfront or the 18th-century streets of the old quarter, where Napoleon grew up; the Maison Bonaparte and the Palais Fesch, with its collection of Renaissance and Baroque art, are the highlights of the old quarter. It's worth venturing further north, where the landscape grows increasingly spectacular as you approach the Golfe de Porto, while further inland, the rivers have created deep and dramatic canyons, such as the Gorges de Spelunca at Evisa and the Gorges du Prunelli near Tolla.

1 Top 10 Sights
p81

1 Restaurants
p87

1 The Best of the Rest
p84

1 Interior Villages
p85

1 Day Walks
p86

For places to stay in this area, see p116

Fishing boats moored in the marina, Ajaccio

1 Ajaccio

A winter livestock market in Roman times, Ajaccio *(p22)* became a major settlement only after the Genoese erected a citadel here in the late 15th century. It expanded rapidly from 1580, and by the mid-17th century had become Corsica's foremost port. Today, it serves as Corsica's main tourist gateway. Above all else, it is famous as being the birthplace of Napoleon, a connection underlined by statues of the "Little Corporal" dominating the town's squares.

2 Plage de Verghia

H4

In Côti-Chiavari, about 40 km (25 miles) south of Ajaccio, this is the least frequented of the sandy bays along the Rive Sud and by far the prettiest. Shallow, crystal-clear water and white sand make it a perfect choice for young families. Pine trees crowning the headland to the west provide shade, and one of the island's more welcoming beach cafés, La Plage d'Argent, serves cold beers on the dune behind.

3 Cala d'Orzu

H4

After the manicured beaches of the Rive Sud, Cala d'Orzu offers a distinct change of tone. The atmosphere here is ruled by the churning waves of nearby Capo di Muro *(p86)*, where a lighthouse surveys a shoreline that feels a million miles away from the Riviera chic of Ajaccio. The bay and its adjacent coves are great for snorkelling and are deserted most weekdays.

4 Cargèse

G1 cargese.corsica

In the 17th century, some 730 refugees from a bloody vendetta in the southern Peloponnese region of Greece alighted on Corsica's west coast near Cargèse. Four hundred years on, their descendants are still here, living in a cluster of neat stone houses set around the village's two churches – one Latin Catholic, one Greek Orthodox. The Greek church, St-Spyridon, holds original icons brought from Mani in 1676, including a 12th-century painting of the Virgin and Child.

5 Plage de Pero

G1

Backed by a scattering of hotels and holiday villas, this well-sheltered bay north of Cargèse makes a great pit stop on long journeys up the west coast. After a dip in its transparent water, stretch your legs with a walk to a 17th-century Genoese watchtower perched on the tip of the headland to the north. Fine views from the tower extend up the coast.

Hiking a trail through the Gorges de Spelunca

8 Piana
A7

Piana has served as the principal springboard for tours to the nearby Calanche rocks since long before the Corniche was surfaced. Its, charming flower-filled 17th-century square continues to attract a steady stream of visitors during the summer months. Although there is nothing much to do here beyond the simple pleasures of penning a postcard or two on a sunny café terrace, explorations of the village's cacti-covered fringes reveal spellbinding vistas of the gulf. If you are here at Easter, do not miss the Granitola procession of hooded penitents, starting at the picturesque Sts-Pierre-et-Paul church.

6 Gorges de Spelunca
B7

The cliffs of the Gorges de Spelunca reach a height of 1,000 m (3,300 ft), soaring above a wild valley carpeted in forest and maquis. You can enjoy the landscape by following the paved trails, or from the depths of a pool in the river on the valley floor.

7 Golfe de Porto

The west coast's prime visitor attraction, the Golfe de Porto (p42) is unique in the Mediterranean for its red porphyry landscapes. The views across the sapphire waters of the bay to the headlands of Capo Rosso and Scandola are unforgettable. Edward Lear, who travelled through the area in 1868, was amazed by its grandeur, rendering the scenery in a series of line drawings.

GENOESE BRIDGES

A typical feature of Corsica's rural landscape are the Genoese bridges over many of its rivers. Although some of these steeply sloping, single-span structures were built in the 1200s, most of them date from the 15th and 16th centuries, when the booming trade in chestnut flour, timber and wine required year-round crossing points.

9 Plage d'Arone

📍 A7

This heavenly beach lies at the foot of a sweep of deserted mountains below Piana and can be reached via the D824. Swimming in turquoise water amid such imposing scenery is an experience that is hard to beat. There is very little else nearby except for a campsite and a few pleasant café-restaurants where you can snack while looking out over the beach. The path winding through the maquis from the north side of the bay leads to a rocky headland, where you can enjoy magnificent views.

10 Capo Rosso

📍 A7

The most southerly of the Herculean red promontories standing guard at the mouth of the Golfe de Porto, Capo Rosso forms a classic humpback shape, its red cliffs rising vertically from the waves to a solitary Genoese watchtower *(p52)*. The panoramic views from the top are unbelievably beautiful, but it is a long, steep climb. Taking around three hours to walk to the top and back, the path starts 7 km (4 miles) west of Piana on the D824.

Admiring the view from Porto marina, Golfe de Porto

A WALK AROUND AJACCIO

Morning

Kick-start your day's sightseeing at one of the workers' cafés fronting the César Campinchi square. From there, follow the narrow backstreet behind the square on to the Rue Fesch, site of the famous **Palais Fesch** *(p23)*. You will need a good couple of hours to work your way around its highlights. Retracing your steps back down the Rue Fesch, emerge at the palm-lined Place Foch. Napoleon aficionados will love the memorabilia in the **Salon Napoléonien** *(p23)*, which is a short walk from the Emperor's birthplace, the **Maison Bonaparte** *(p23)*, where you can see the divan on which he was born. Nearby, the **A Casetta** deli is one of the city's best Corsican-produce shops, selling fine charcuterie, sardines, wines and honey.

Afternoon

Pause for lunch at one of the restaurants on the **Port Tino Rossi**, then follow the road skirting the Genoese **Citadelle** *(p23)* and St François beach until you see the **Ajaccio Cathedral** *(p22)* on your right, worth a visit for its evocative Delacroix painting. A short walk from there across the **Place de Gaulle**, dominated by a statue of Napoleon and his brothers, brings you to Ajaccio's main shopping street, **Cours Napoléon**. Afterwards, tuck into a traditional gourmet Corsican meal at **Le Don Quichotte** *(p87)*.

The Best of the Rest

Wild flowers bordering the beach at Portigliolo

1. A Cupulatta
📍 J2 🏠 Vignola, Vero, Ucciuni, 17 km (11 miles) NE of Ajaccio 🕐 Apr–mid-May & mid-Sep–mid-Nov: 10am–5pm daily; mid-May–mid-Sep: 9am–6pm daily 🌐 acupulatta.com 📱

This sanctuary is home to a great collection of tortoises and other reptiles, from Jurassic-looking giants to teeny terrapins. It is 30 minutes northeast of Ajaccio on the N193.

2. Porticcio
📍 H3
The largest of the Rive Sud's ribbon of resorts, Porticcio is centred on a broad, sandy beach. Take a bus from Ajaccio or a boat from the old port.

3. Portigliolo
📍 H4
This idyllic, semi-circular bay at the southwestern extremity of the Golfe d'Ajaccio has a laid-back beach and a well-sheltered snorkelling spot.

4. Golfe de Sagone
📍 H2
Dip your toes in the water of the spectacular beach at Sagone, on the next gulf up the coast from Ajaccio.

5. Plage de Bussaglia
📍 B6
If you are in the Porto area and keen to avoid the crowds, this curve of pebbles and blue water is the best option.

6. Col de Vergio
📍 C6
To enjoy the dramatic forests and mountains, head up to the rock-strewn "Pass of the Virgin", dividing the Spelunca and Niolo gorges.

7. Le Bélvèdere, Forêt d'Aïtone
📍 C7
This natural balcony formed by boulders at the head of the Gorges de Spelunca is a great starting point for walks through the Forêt d'Aïtone.

8. Plage de Chiuni
📍 B7
An amazingly secluded bay, Chiuni has a small holiday complex.

9. Plage de Gradelle
📍 A6
Sublime sunset views across the gulf to Capo d'Orto and the Calanche are the chief asset of this beach, northwest of the Golfe de Porto.

10. Pont de Zaglia
📍 B7
This Genoese bridge is where walkers following the trail from Evisa to Ota (*p62*) come for a spot of swimming.

Crossing the medieval Genoese Pont de Zaglia

Houses with slate roofs overlooking Lac de Tolla

Interior Villages

1. Vico
📍 H1

To escape the tourist trail completely, head 15 km (9 miles) inland from Sagone to Vico, where the medieval, café-lined square offers plenty of shade and a peaceful atmosphere.

2. Tolla
📍 J2

For a total change of vibe from Ajaccio, head east up the Gorges du Prunelli to Tolla, a quaint granite village overlooking a huge spread of lake and craggy mountains.

3. Marignana
📍 B7

Marignana's pretty cluster of red-tiled houses with old stone balconies jutting over the chestnut canopy comes as a heavenly vision for walkers on this region's trails

4. Soccia
📍 C7

The tarmac comes to an end at Soccia, a breathtaking mountain village from where ancient mule tracks, now used by walkers, lead to the surrounding ridges and forests.

5. Renno
📍 B7

A bastion of traditional Corsican hill culture, Renno is one of the island's remotest settlements. Each February, the annual fair, A Tumbera, celebrates the pig and all its uses in Corsican cuisine.

6. Revinda
📍 B7

Corsica's smallest permanently inhabited village is on a lonely hillside above Cargèse *(p81)*. Aside from the views, the main attraction is nearby refuge E Case.

7. Guagno-les-Bains
📍 J1

Pascal Paoli was among the patrons of the spa in this village in the Sagone hinterland. The thermal, sulphurous waters here were a sought-after cure for rheumatic and skin disorders.

8. Evisa
📍 B7

Chestnut trees and the age-old traditions of pig rearing govern life in this picturesque hill village above the Gorges de Spelunca – popular as much for its cuisine as its forest walks.

9. Ota
📍 B6

Clinging to a steep, maquis-covered hillside above Porto, this classic mountain village of 17th-century granite houses boasts stupendous views across the valley to the north cliffs of Capo d'Orto *(p86)*.

10. Côti-Chiavari
📍 H4

An unforgettable panorama of sea and mountains unfolds from Côti-Chiavari. Its pale-grey houses, reached via a series of switchbacks from the Rive Sud, straddle high above the Golfe d'Ajaccio.

Day Walks

1. Capo d'Orto
B7

An immense 360-degree panorama over Corsica's most sublime landscape is the reward for ascending Capo d'Orto, the sugar-loaf summit looming dramatically above Porto.

2. Ota to Serriera
B6

One of the benchmark stages of the Tra Mare e Monti Nord trail (p63), this route winds over the 900-m- (2,950-ft-) high San Petru pass.

3. Evisa to Marignana
B7

This leisurely amble through the woodland makes for an ideal day-long walk. Stop for lunch at Ustaria di a Rota.

4. Col de Vergio to Cascades de Radule
C6

An immensely enjoyable hike over the rocky terrain of the upper Golo Valley brings you to a blue-green pool fed by a perennial waterfall.

5. Col de la Croix to Girolata

This three-hour hike takes you from the Golfe de Porto's Corniche to the coastal village of Girolata (p42), via the dense maquis and a beautiful cove.

Hiker taking a break en route to the Capo d'Orto

6. Château Fort
B7

A colossal chunk of red porphyry that resembles a castle, the Château Fort marks the end point of an hour-long jaunt north of the Roches Bleues café, through the Calanche rock formations.

7. Sentier Muletier
B7

A small oratory in the cliff, 500 m (1,640 ft) south of the Roches Bleues café, flags the head of this tougher trail through the Calanche via the path that connects Ota and Piana.

8. Evisa to Pont de Zaglia
B7

Follow a zigzagging medieval track, with original cobbles intact, through chestnut and oak forest to this Genoese packhorse bridge (p84), where you can bathe in the river.

9. Chemin des Crêtes
H3

A superb ridge route, the Chemin des Crêtes heads uphill from Ajaccio, following the rocky spine of the mountain that rises behind the city.

10. Capo di Muro
H4

This is the nearest stretch of wild coast if you track the shoreline south from Ajaccio. An old watchtower makes the perfect target for a leisurely walk along the headland.

Restaurants

Diners enjoying Corsican cuisine at Le 20123

1. Le Don Quichotte

⚐ P2 ⌂ 6 Rue des Halles, Ajaccio 🕐 Sun Ⓦ ledonquichotte.fr · €€

Dine on creative Corsican cuisine at this brasserie. Specialities include beef tartare and sumptuous desserts.

2. A Nepita

⚐ H3 ⌂ 4 Rue San Lazaro, Ajaccio 🕐 Mon & Sun Ⓦ anepita.fr · €€€

The modern menu changes daily and features local fish and meat, plus excellent wines. Book ahead.

3. Le 20123

⚐ P3 ⌂ 2 Rue du Roi de Rome, Ajaccio 🕐 Noon–2pm & 7–11pm Mon–Sat, 7–11pm Sun 🕐 Nov–Apr: Mon Ⓦ 20123.fr · €€

Dine on traditional rural cuisine in the re-created hamlet of Pina Canale.

4. Les Roches Rouges

⚐ A7 ⌂ Piana, Golfe de Porto 🕐 Mon & Tue; Nov–Apr Ⓦ lesrochesrouges.com · €€€

Gourmet cuisine is served in a *fin-de-siècle* dining hall with sublime views.

5. Le Bélvèdere

⚐ H4 ⌂ Côti-Chiavari 🕐 Mar–mid-Nov: 7:30–9pm daily; Mar–May: noon–2:30pm Sun Ⓦ lebelvedere decoti.com · €€

Set in a bed-and-breakfast, high above the Rive Sud, this restaurant has fantastic views from its terrace.

6. L'Altru Versu

⚐ H3 ⌂ Les Sept Chapelles, Route des Sanguinaires, Ajaccio 📞 04955 00522 🕐 9am–3pm & 6–10pm Tue–Sun 🕐 Winter · €€€

This restaurant, offering a refined, gourmet take on traditional Corsican cuisine, is the first choice for foodies.

7. A Casa Corsa, Piana

⚐ A7 ⌂ Route de Porto 🕐 7am–10pm daily Ⓦ acasacorsa-piana.com · €€

Choose your own lobster at this fresh seafood restaurant offering sunset views of the Calanche de Piana.

8. L'Arbousier

⚐ H3 ⌂ Hotel Le Maquis, 585 Boulevard Marie-Jeanne Bozzi, Porticcio 🕐 Jan–Feb Ⓦ lemaquis.com/fr · €€€

High Gallic gastronomy, made from local ingredients by chef Gérard Lorenzoni-Salini, is served here.

9. A Tramula (Bar de la Poste)

⚐ B7 ⌂ Rue Capo Soprano, Evisa 📞 04952 30894 🕐 11:30am–9:30pm daily (Oct–mid-Apr: by reservation only) · €€€

Relish the charcuterie, veal and other delights on offer here. Ask for a table on the balcony to enjoy great views.

10. A Merendella Citadina

⚐ P3 ⌂ 19 Rue Conventionnel Chiappe, Ajaccio 🕐 Mon & Tue Ⓦ a-merendella-citadina-restaurant-ajaccio.fr · €€

Charcuterie, *figatellu* (local sausage), roasted goat and sautéed veal with chestnut honey are among the specialities at this restaurant.

BONIFACIO AND THE SOUTH

The resort town of Bonifacio was built in the 9th century to defend the coast against pirates. The town is today known for its busy marina, medieval attractions and clifftop Citadelle, but its the striking natural setting that is most remarkable. Bonifacio's chalk cliffs rise abruptly from the Mediterranean, with the town perched vertiginously on top. With a picturesque port surrounded by wild maquis, the town has an otherworldly atmosphere. Not far from Bonifacio is Porto-Vecchio, where the shore is strung with magnificent beaches, such as the famous Palombaggia, and the streets are lined with bars and restaurants. Inland, a giant wall of hills and dense pine forest separates the coast from the rugged landscapes of Alta Rocca, which sprawl into the Golfe de Valinco below the skyline of Sartène.

1 Top 10 Sights
p89

1 Places to Eat
p93

1 The Best of the Rest
p92

For places to stay in this area, see p116

1 Pianu di Levie (Cucuruzzu)

◎ K4 📍 17 km (11 miles) SW of Zonza 🕐 Apr–Oct: 9:30am–6pm daily (Jun–Sep: to 7pm) 🌐 isula.corsica ↗

Savour the atmosphere and distinctive landscape of the Alta Rocca region from the ramparts of this Bronze Age castle, with its vaulted chambers, stairways, hearths and granaries. The site, inhabited around 1400 BCE, is set amid an ancient holm oak forest, with views of the distant Aiguilles de Bavella. A 20-minute walk north leads to the A Capula, occupied until 1259, where a Romanesque chapel stands in a clearing. Don't miss Levie's fascinating museum *(p47)*, which explores the evolution of prehistoric civilization on the island. From November to March, it is open for group bookings only.

2 Porto-Vecchio

◎ L5

The Genoese developed Porto-Vecchio in 1539 as a harbour from which to ship Corsican cork to the Italian mainland. Afflicted by malaria-carrying mosquitoes, it was eventually abandoned, but has seen a resurgence since World War II, owing to its proximity to some of the island's finest beaches. Chic boutiques pitched at high-rolling Italians line the *haute ville's* medieval streets, which converge at the St Jean-Baptiste and the cheerful Place de la République, filled with cafés and ice-cream shops.

3 Îles Lavezzi

◎ L7

This cluster of low granite-rock islets off Bonifacio rests amid superbly transparent water. Boats shuttle here throughout the day in the high season, allowing plenty of time for snorkelling and for exploring the archipelago's winding pathways and hidden coves. The only structures of note are the walled Cimetière Archiano, where victims of the 1855 shipwreck of the *Sémillante (p31)* are buried, and a memorial to the disaster. Bring refreshments along, as there are no cafés on the islands.

Dining at a café in a quaint alleyway, Sartène

4 Sartène

The playwright Prosper Mérimée famously dubbed Sartène as "the most Corsican of Corsican towns" – though whether he was referring to its austere appearance or the grim-faced demeanour of its inhabitants is a moot point. Enjoy an apéritif on the ancient place Porta, where locals congregate for a postprandial walk, then wander around the narrow back alleys. The town's museum has the island's largest collection of prehistoric artifacts.

5 Alta Rocca

◎ K4

The hilly interior of southern Corsica is known as the Alta Rocca. With its deep river valleys, lush chestnut and oak forests and ancient granite villages, it is a world away from the coast. The old paved mule trails and the Mare a Mare Sud hiking route *(p62)* are a great way to explore the area, but you can also cover the highlights in a day-long driving tour, stopping for swims, woodland strolls and charcuterie along the way.

6 Plage de Palombaggia
🗺 L6

The turquoise water and soft white sand at Palombaggia make for a picture-perfect setting. The pristine beach here actually comprises three contiguous bays, separated by headlands crowned by clumps of umbrella and maritime pines. Palombaggia is the most northerly of the trio and the best for watersports; next comes Tamaricciu, with its stylish café-restaurant made of teak; and finally, Accario, the smallest and quietest.

7 Bonifacio

On a narrow precipice high over the blue waters of the Straits, this old Genoese town (p30) withstood repeated sieges by the Aragonese and, in 1554, a Turkish fleet led by the corsair Dragut (p43). The dramatic harbour, clifftop Citadelle and chalk escarpments bring visitors year round. From July to September, its cobbled alleyways are often overrun with daytrippers – all the more reason to take an excursion boat out of the port below to view the *haute ville* from sea level.

8 Golfe de Valinco

The serene beaches on both the northern and southern shores of the Golfe de Valinco (p26) are the main reason people base themselves in the southwest of the island, but there are many interesting sights inland to tempt you away from the coast – not least the famous prehistoric site of Filitosa. Catch an excursion boat from Propriano to explore this area's wild coves. Look out for the Genoese watchtowers, a legacy of

GROUPER FISH

The clear waters in the Straits of Bonifacio are home to a large colony of extraordinary fish. Tamed by decades of visits, the shoal of grouper used to take morsels from divers' hands, a practice that has been banned. The colony is protected as part of the Réserve Naturelle des Bouches de Bonifacio.

**Shallow turquoise waters
at Plage de Palombaggia**

the pirate raids that forced the local
population into the hills in the 15th
and 16th centuries.

9 Route de Bavella
◻ L3

One of Corsica's most scenic roads,
the Route de Bavella winds inland from
Solenzara on the southeast coast,
approaching the Aiguilles via a series
of cliffs, forests and gorges. Despite
attempts to widen the road, slow-
moving vehicles impede progress in
high season, so try to get an early start.

10 Aiguilles de Bavella
◻ K4

Rising from the Corsican watershed
on the opposite side of the valley
from Monte Incudine, the Aiguilles
de Bavella are giant towers of granite.
The stacks are visible for miles around,
lending a serrated appearance to
the skyline inland from Porto-Vecchio.
Yellow waymarks flag a scrambling
route up to and around the bases – a
variant of the GR20 trekking trail, for
which the needles provide a stunning
closing stretch.

**Hiking the GR20 trail through
the Aiguilles de Bavella**

ROUTE DE BAVELLA AND MASSIF DE L'OSPÉDALE

Morning

This driving tour takes in the scenic
highlights of the mountain area
inland from **Porto-Vecchio** (*p89*).
Leave town on the main Bastia
road (T10) and follow it as far as
Solenzara, winding southwest
above the Solenzara river. A
panorama of mountains is
revealed at the **Col de Larone**.
From there onwards, the
landscape grows more spectacular
at each bend. In the shadow of the
famous **Aiguilles de Bavella**, you
can follow a waymarked trail
through pine forest to the **Trou de
la Bombe** (*p63*), before refuelling
with a Corsican lunch at the
Auberge du Col de Bavella (*p93*).

Afternoon

A white **Notre-Dame-des-Neiges**
(Our Lady of the Snow) statue
presides over the high point of the
pass, from where the D268 winds
downhill all the way to **Zonza**
(*p50*). From Zonza, follow the
D368 into the wooded Massif
de l'Ospédale. Beyond the
Bocca d'Illarata pass, a café on
the left side of the road marks
the start of a 90-minute
walk to the 70-m (230-ft)
Piscia di Gallu waterfall. At
Ospédale, the next village on
the D368, **A Tigliola** restaurant
has superb views across
to Sardinia.

Ermitage de la Trinité set amid massive granite boulders

The Best of the Rest

1. Piantarella
⏹ L7
This kayaking, kitesurfing and sailboarding hot spot to the east of Bonifacio encompasses the clearest water on the island.

2. Plage de Pinarello
⏹ L5
Shallow, pale-blue water, enfolded by a crescent of white sand, makes Pinarello a most attractive beach for families. Easily accessible by road, it gets busy in peak season.

3. Quenza
⏹ K4
Over 1,000 years old, this is a quintessential Alta Rocca village, where the broad-leaf forest ebbs into the high uplands of the Coscione plateau. A chapel stands on its outskirts.

4. Plateau de Coscione
⏹ K3
To the north of the Alta Rocca, this upland served as a summer pasture for the region's shepherds for centuries. It now lies deserted, save for the odd walker and horse rider.

5. Carbini
⏹ K5
Carbini, at the foot of the Massif de l'Ospédale, is the site of the Pisan church of San Giovanni where, in 1362, a heretical sect was slaughtered on the orders of the Pope.

6. Cala di l'Avena
⏹ H6
A broad bay lashed by surf, Cala di l'Avena is ideal if you like wild and windy beaches. A no-frills campsite behind it provides the essentials.

7. Plage de Tralicetu
⏹ J6
You have to negotiate a very rough, 4-km (3-mile) track to reach Tralicetu, one of southern Corsica's most remote and unspoiled beaches.

8. Castellu d'Araggio
⏹ L5
Perched high on a rocky hillside to the northwest of Porto-Vecchio, this prehistoric citadel enjoys a spectacular setting. It offers magnificent views extending across the coast.

9. Plage de Balistra
⏹ L6
This is the only beach in the Porto-Vecchio–Bonifacio area where you can be assured plenty of room even at the height of summer. Brave the badly rutted piste to get here.

10. Ermitage de la Trinité
⏹ K7
Huddled beneath a huge granite outcrop, the Ermitage de la Trinité is among the oldest Christian monuments on Corsica. A superb vista extends down the coast.

Places to Eat

1. Cantina Doria
📍 K7 🏠 27 Rue Doria, Bonifacio
📞 06199 20083 🕐 Nov–Apr · €€
Enjoy quality Corsican cuisine, in this restaurant, squeezed into an alley in the *haute ville*.

2. Les Quatre Vents
📍 K7 🏠 29 Quai Banda del Ferro, Bonifacio 🕐 Noon–2pm & 7pm–10pm Sun–Fri 🌐 restaurant-les-quatre-vents-bonifacio.fr · €€
Some of Bonifacio's best seafood and bouillabaisse are served in this restaurant overlooking the water. Booking is essential in high season.

3. Tamaricciu
📍 L6 🏠 Plage Palombaggia, Porto-Vecchio 🕐 9am–10pm daily (to 10:30pm Mon) 🌐 tamaricciu.com · €€€
This beach bistro is known for fresh salads, pasta dishes, wood-grilled fish and (at lunchtime) pizzas.

4. Casadelmar
📍 L5 🏠 Rte de Palombaggia, near Porto-Vecchio 🕐 Hours vary, check website 🌐 casadelmar.fr · €€€
Sample the culinary delights crafted by two-Michelin-starred chef Fabio Bragagnolo here.

5. Le Lido
📍 J5 🏠 42 Av Napoléon III, Propriano 🕐 Late Oct–Apr 🌐 lelidohotel.com · €€€
The spectacular views here are matched by the food, with fresh, creative takes on island classics.

6. Bergerie d'Acciola
📍 J5 🏠 Orasi, route de Bonifacio, 8 km (5 miles) S of Sartène 📞 04957 71400 🕐 Oct–May · €€
This popular terrace restaurant is known for its excellent regional food. The dishes made with local ewe's and goat's cheese are recommended.

7. Auberge du Col de Bavella
📍 L4 🏠 Col de Bavella, Zonza 🕐 Nov–Mar 🌐 auberge-bavella.com · €€
Walkers on the GR20 stop here to refuel with homemade stew, charcuterie, grilled lamb and tasty desserts.

8. Jardin de l'Échaugette
📍 J5 🏠 Place Vardiola, Rue Petrajo, Sartène 📞 06204 07149 🕐 Oct–early Apr · €€
Enjoy specialities such as veal stew with chestnut polenta at this restaurant.

9. U Sirenu
📍 J5 🏠 Orasi, Route de Bonifacio, Sartène 🌐 usirenu.fr · €€
The setting is gorgeous, the terrace lovely and the local Corsican grilled meats succulent. There is a pool, too.

10. A Pignata
📍 K4 🏠 Route du Pianu, Levie 📞 04957 84190 🕐 Dec–Mar · €€
Enjoy splendid views across the Alta Rocca and rustic cooking at this farmhouse. Booking is essential.

Enjoying a hearty breakfast at Le Lido

CORTE, THE INTERIOR AND THE EAST COAST

If you never venture from the coast, your impression of Corsica will be distorted. Inland, the deep, forested valleys of the island's core create a radical shift in tone. Spilling from the foot of a citadel, Corte is the largest town in Corsica's interior. Its *haute ville*, a warren of red-tiled tenements and churches, presides over a nexus of several major valleys, making it the perfect springboard for treks into the mountains. The quickest route to Corte is via Aléria on the east coast. It has impressive Roman ruins, mountain villages and a vast expanse of relatively unfrequented beaches.

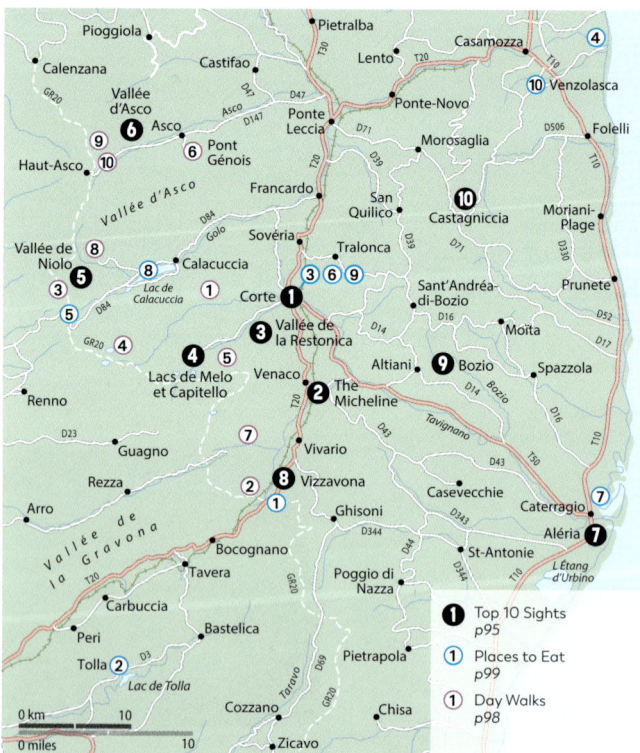

Top 10 Sights
p95

Places to Eat
p99

Day Walks
p98

For places to stay in this area, see p116

The town of Corte high in the mountainous interior

1 Corte
Corte (p40) served as the island's capital between 1755 and 1769, when Pascal Paoli made it the seat of his revolutionary government. With its imposing mountain backdrop and Moor's Head flags above an 18th-century old town, Corte still retains an aura of nationalist defiance. Bullet holes made by Genoese besiegers pockmark the walls of the cobbled square below the Citadelle, where Corsican-speaking students from the nearby university crowd the bars in term time.

2 The Micheline
Known affectionately as the "Micheline", Corsica's little train is an essential, year-round, all-weather link between Ajaccio and Bastia. The route, built in the 19th century and upgraded in 2008, is breathtakingly scenic – especially the stretch branching northwest to Calvi from Ponte Leccia, which skirts the fabulous Balagne coastline. Catch one of the four daily services to Vizzavona from Corte – a 50-minute ride through pine forests and pretty villages, including a crossing of the famous Pont de Vecchio bridge.

3 Vallée de la Restonica
D6
Mesmerized by the high ridges above them, few visitors to the Vallée de la Restonica spare more than a passing glance at the valley floor, but the river surging across it hides dozens of swimming spots. The meltwater cascades through pools hollowed from granite boulders called "vasques". Shady areas under the Laricio pines make perfect picnic spots, while a network of trails provides a great opportunity for a walk around the forest.

4 Lacs de Melo et Capitello
C7
The Vallée de la Restonica scythes from the outskirts of Corte into the heart of the watershed – one of the Mediterranean's great mountain wildernesses. In summer, visitors drive or catch the shuttle bus to the car park at the end of the valley, from where a trail leads to two beautiful glacial lakes. Visit before the snow melts in early May to see the lakes partly frozen.

5 Vallée de Niolo
C6
Corsica's most remote mountain region is the Vallée de Niolo. Its focal point, below the eroded southern fringes of Monte Cinto (p61), is a broad depression scattered with granite villages where vestiges of the old transhumant culture that once held sway here are still discernible. The local ewe's cheese is mouth-wateringly good, and the walking is superlative. If you are in the area in September, do not miss the annual fair, A Santa di u Niolu (p75).

6 Vallée d'Asco
📍 C5

The head of the Asco Valley, known as Haut-Asco, is flanked by Corsica's highest mountains, including Monte Cinto. It was here, amid the pines and boulder moraines, that Felix von Cube and the other early pioneers of Corsican mountaineering made their base camp in the 1900s, while forging routes up the peaks. The wood-lined bar in the ski station here displays antique photos of the explorers and you can admire the awesome crags opposite from Le Chalet's terrace.

7 Aléria
📍 M1

At the mouth of the Tavignano river on the eastern coastal plain, Aléria was a major Greek and Roman colony in ancient times, when the Étang de Diane lagoon below was the island's main harbour and naval base. Ruins of the former Roman town *(closed Sun in Oct–May)*, which include baths, a forum, triumphal archway and archaeological museum, are spread over a hilltop to the south of the modern village. Foodies can dine on oysters from the nearby *étang* (pond).

Ancient ruins in the Roman settlement of Aléria

L'Agnone river flowing under a bridge, Vizzavona

8 Vizzavona
📍 K1

A collection of tin-roofed railway buildings and forestry huts, Vizzavona is the highest stop on Corsica's diminutive train line. Picnickers meander through the woods to the Cascade des Anglais *(p98)*, while those with more stamina and a head for heights scale the Monte d'Oro, whose cliffs and summit are this area's defining landmark.

9 Bozio
📍 L1

This micro-region, overlooking the Vallée du Tavignano *(p40)* to the southeast of Corte, sees very few visitors but is a great area for getting a feel of traditional mountain life. Along

what was the old Via Romana, a string of picturesque stone villages looks across the valley to Monte Rotondo. The Mare a Mare Centre hiking trail winds through deserted uplands and ruined sheepfolds.

10 Castagniccia
E5

Swathed in a dense canopy of chestnut forest, Castagniccia, in the northeast of the island, has an entirely different feel to it. The intense greenery ensures a moist climate and in autumn, when the woods are ablaze with colour, mist cloaks the valley floor most mornings. Splendid Baroque churches, great walks around the forest and the pungent local charcuterie draw visitors here.

CORSICAN POLYPHONY

Corsica has its own distinctive brand of choral music – known locally as "polyphonies corses". The style, which hinges on three or four parts, evolved as a means of singing Mass in remote shepherds' villages, but has since become the backbone of a vibrant and popular musical revival led by groups such as I Muvrini and A Filetta (p77).

A DRIVE THROUGH CORSICA'S INTERIOR

Morning

This circular route loops through some of the least visited, but most scenic corners of central and eastern Corsica. Begin by heading south from **Corte** (p40) on the main Ajaccio highway (T20). After 33 km (21 miles), just beyond Vivario, turn left on to the D69 at the **Col de la Serra Piana** (p98) to start the ascent of the 1311-m- (4,300-ft-) high **Col de Sorba**. An 11-km (7-mile) drop down the other side brings you to the village of **Ghisoni**, where there's a great café, **A Stazzona** (Jun–Sep), to make an atmospheric pit stop. From Ghisoni, follow the D344 as it winds through the awesome **Défilé de Strette** gorge to Ste-Antoine, where you should follow the D343 to **Aléria**. Tour the hilltop Roman ruins before heading to the **Plage du Padulone**. Then continue northwest from Aléria on the T50, turning right on to the D14 after 13 km (8 miles).

Afternoon

This road follows the old Via Romana through the **Bozio** region – among the most spectacular drives on the island. Head through Pietraserena, Altiani and Erbajolo villages, before descending to the valley via the D14. This brings you to the T50, only 5 km (3 miles) south of Corte.

Traversing the beautiful landscape of Lac d'Oriente

Day Walks

1. Gorges du Tavignano
📍 C7

Follow the zigzagging Genoese mule track up this valley near Corte to reach an awesome gorge, carpeted with Laricio pines. Chanterelle mushrooms grow in profusion here in autumn.

2. Cascade des Anglais
📍 K1

Accessed via a gentle 20-minute amble through a pine forest, this idyllic waterfall is a perfect spot for a picnic, with plenty of pools to splash about in nearby.

3. Cascades de Radule
📍 C6

The landscape starts to feel like a mountain as you approach the hidden Radule waterfall, just off the GR20 in the Golo river valley. The start point is the car park at Col de Vergio.

4. Lac de Nino
📍 C7

Scramble up the steep sides of the Vallée de Niolo to reach the largest and most beautiful of Corsica's many glacial lakes, suspended in the middle of green pasture, against a magnificent mountain backdrop.

5. Lac d'Oriente
📍 D7

The challenging climb up Monte Rotondo may be only for confirmed mountaineering enthusiasts, but this magical glacial lake halfway up is more easily accessible.

6. Col de la Serra Piana
📍 D5

Swim under the old Pont d'Asco Genoese bridge before climbing the side valley opposite Asco village to reach a lonely pass with great views.

7. Gorges de Manganellu
📍 D7

Follow the orange waymarks from the hamlet of Canaglia, 25 km (16 miles) south of Corte, to reach one of the island's loveliest forested valleys. The remote Bergerie de Tolla is the perfect turnaround point.

8. Pont de Muricciolu
📍 C6

On the outskirts of Albertacce village, a Genoese packhorse bridge spans a particularly photogenic stretch of river. Huge, water-worn slabs flank the river, which you can reach in an easy half-hour's walk.

9. Punta Muvrella
📍 C5

The "Peak of the Sheep" is a superb eagle's nest summit overlooking the Vallée d'Asco (p96) to the Cinto Massif. It is a relentlessly steep three-hour, 700-m (2,296-ft) climb from the Haut-Asco ski station.

10. Tour des Cinque Frati
📍 C6

This is a classic walk in the Vallée de Niolo (p95), looping around a phalanx of rock pinnacles. Leaflets detailing the route are on sale at local tourist offices.

Places to Eat

1. Monte d'Oro
📍 K1 🏠 Vivario, near Vizzavona
🕐 Oct–Apr 🌐 monte-oro.com · €€
Try traditional mountain cooking at this famous wayside restaurant, where the main Ajaccio–Bastia highway crosses the watershed.

2. Bergerie de Tolla
📍 K1 🏠 Gorges de Manganellu
🕐 Late Sep–early Jun · €
This sheepfold in the forest serves delicious ewe's cheese omelettes.

3. Auberge de la Restonica
📍 D6 🏠 Route de Restonica, 2 km (1 mile) SW of Corte 🕐 Nov–Mar
🌐 restaurant-corte.fr · €€
Quality Corsican mountain cuisine, such as fresh trout stuffed with mint, is served at this romantic hotel.

4. U Fragnu
📍 F5 🏠 U Campu, Route de Vescovato, Venzolasca 📞 04953 66233 🕐 Oct · €€
This bistro, specializing in Corsican cuisine, serves huge portions of veal and olive stew and *brocciu* fritters.

5. "U Cintu" Chez Jojo
📍 C6 🏠 Albertacce, Vallée de Niolo 📞 04954 80687 · €
Sample charcuterie, rich game stews and chestnut flour desserts in this restaurant next to the Calacuccia lake.

6. A Casa di l'Orsu
📍 D7 🏠 4 Rue Mgr Sauveur Casanova, Corte 📞 06621 550765 · €€
Enjoy traditional Corsican cuisine at A Casa di l'Orsu, which also has a wide range of vegan and vegetarian options.

7. Aux Coquillages de Diana
📍 M1 🏠 Étang de Diana, Aléria
📞 04955 70455 · €€
Shellfish aficionados can tuck into local Nustale oysters and mussels, washed down with Vermentino wine.

8. Restaurant l'Ampugnani
📍 E5 🏠 La Porta, Castagniccia
🕐 11:30am–10pm daily 🌐 ampugnani.com · €€
Savour Castagniccian trout, delicious free-range pork stews and crunchy *brocciu beignets* in this dining salon that also offers lovely valley views.

9. Osteria di l'Orta
📍 D6 🏠 Casa Guelfucci, Pont de l'Orta, Corte 🕐 Oct–Mar 🌐 osteria-di-l-orta.com· €€
Corsican specialities, such as veal with olives and a chestnut mousse, entice diners to this restaurant in an 18th-century mansion.

10. L'Ortu
📍 F5 🏠 Route de Venzolasca, Vescovato 📞 06496 55196
🕐 Oct–Apr · €€
This organic farm-restaurant specializes in vegetarian fare made with its organic and locally sourced produce. A wide variety of free-range pork dishes are on the menu for meat lovers.

The rustic interior of U Fragnu bistro

BASTIA AND THE NORTH

With its rugged interior and turquoise water-fringed coastline, the far north of Corsica, stretching from Bastia to Calvi via Cap Corse, confirms most of the clichés usually ascribed to the island. There is barely a patch of flat ground in the entire region. Journeys tend to be winding and take longer than you would expect, but reveal astonishing landscapes at every bend. The Italian influence is slightly more marked in the north too, especially around Bastia, where the Genoese-built Vieux Port could have been transported in its entirety from the Ligurian coast, visible on clear days across the Tyrrhenian Sea. The Genoese were also responsible for the most striking human-made landmark of the far north: Calvi's Citadelle, whose ochre walls preside over a magnificent panorama of sea and granite mountains.

Around Corbara

1 Top 10 Sights
p101

1 Places to Eat
p105

1 The Best of the Rest
p104

For places to stay in this area, see p116

Beautifully illuminated Bastia overlooking the Vieux Port

1 Bastia

Bastia *(p32)* is the island's main centre of commerce and culture. Despite the fact that Napoleon made his home town Ajaccio the official capital, Bastia has a more citified atmosphere than its rival. For visitors, the Vieux Port district of Terra Vecchia, and the Citadelle district of Terra Nova overlooking it, form the principal focus. The Second Empire thoroughfares across town have many places to shop.

2 Patrimonio

The Genoese exported vast quantities of wine from Patrimonio – mostly sweet, blossom-scented muscat. A few thousand hectares of vines remain under cultivation on the leeward side of the village's striking chalk escarpments, although today Patrimonio is synonymous with its superb dry reds. In the shadow of the village church, numerous wine *caves* offer tastings.

3 Pigna

📍 C4

The striking sky-blue woodwork and immaculately pointed stone masonry testify to Pigna's government-funded renaissance as a centre for local arts and crafts. A dozen or more studios operate here, selling ceramics, musical boxes, bamboo flutes and Corsican citterns, among other things. Pigna's main hotel-restaurant, Casa Musicale *(p105)* is a major centre for traditional Balagne music.

4 Erbalunga

📍 F3

Only 9 km (6 miles) north of Bastia, the fishing port of Erbalunga has almost become a suburb of the city – albeit one with a distinct identity of its own. The picturesque harbour's entrance is guarded by a stalwart watchtower, and Le Pirate restaurant *(p105)* nearby serves excellent seafood. Erbalunga is also known across the island for its sombre Good Friday procession of masked penitents, La Cerca *(p74)*, a sight well worth catching if you are in the area.

5 Calvi

Calvi's spectacular setting *(p38)* has lured visitors since the early days of tourism in the region. Its attractions include a marina, a few Baroque churches and the house claimed locally to be the birthplace of Christopher Columbus. The highlight is the Genoese Citadelle, framed by its backdrop of brilliant-blue sea and mountains.

6 Sant'Antonino

C4

The constellation of pastel-washed, orange- and pink-granite villages strewn over the hillsides immediately inland from L'Île Rousse and Calvi – an area known as the Balagne – are ranked among the prettiest in the Mediterranean; and Sant'Antonino is widely regarded as the most picturesque of them all. Its warren of narrow, cobbled alleyways crowd like a bird's nest on the conical summit of a hill, affording visitors a dramatic panoramic view of the surrounding sea and hills.

CAP CORSE MUSCAT

The famous muscat wine, produced in the wonderful vineyards of Cap Corse, is made from a sweet, aromatic grape and has been a speciality of the region since Genoese times. The fruit is partially sun-dried to intensify the sugars before being pressed. Fermentation occurs later with an infusion of pure alcohol.

Buildings in the town of St-Florent along the harbour

7 Giunssani

C5

Given its proximity to the Balagne coast, it is amazing how few visitors venture into the beautiful Giunssani region, just over the mountain from L'Île Rousse. A hidden Shangri-La of chestnut and pine forest, crashing streams and wonderful scenery, the region is dominated by the awesome profile of the 2,393-m- (7,850-ft-) high Monte Padro to the south.

8 Cap Corse

Plunging sheer into the sea, the western flank of the Cap Corse peninsula is steep and relatively inhospitable, with schist-roofed hamlets clinging to the few balconies of level land above tiny harbours. The eastern side, however, has a gentler feel. Terraced vineyards, founded five centuries ago by the Genoese, cascade to a slither of undulating shoreline. It takes a day to round the cape by car, an experience not to be missed.

9 St-Florent

The absence of a white-sand beach within easy driving distance of the town has left the cluster of slate-tiled

A DRIVE AROUND THE CAP CORSE CORNICHE

fisher's houses packed around St-Florent's Citadelle delightfully unspoiled. There are some magnificent beaches across the gulf, such as the Plage du Lotu, but you have to jump on a boat to get to them. The waterfront, lined with cafés, is truly atmospheric at sunset, when the Tenda hills behind turn molten red.

10 L'Île Rousse
🗺 C4

Founded by Pascal Paoli in 1765, L'Île Rousse has thrived ever since, particularly after its rebirth as a French Riviera-style resort. Midway along the Balagne coast, the red isle rises to the north, and a superb view extends from its lighthouse across the rooftops to the hills beyond.

Morning
A circuit of the Corniche can be completed in a full day. Begin by heading out of **Bastia** (*p32*) on the D81, which crosses the ridge at windswept Col de Teghime. Stop for a coffee and croissant in the **Place des Portes** (*p37*) in **St-Florent** then proceed northwards through the vineyards of **Patrimonio** towards **Nonza** (*p104*), where the Genoese watchtower affords another stupendous view – this time west over the bay to the Désert des Agriate coast. The shoreline grows noticeably wilder as you press north. Pause at pretty **Centuri Port** (*p35*) for a stroll around its little lobster-fishing harbour, then begin the zigzagging ascent of the Cap's northern tip to reach Barcaggio via the D253. Stop for lunch at the **U Fanale** restaurant.

Afternoon
From Barcaggio, continue west to **Macinaggio** (*p34*), from where excursion boats run up the wild coastline further north. The remaining leg down the east coast of the Cap is an easier drive; be sure to stock up on fine muscat at the **Domaine Pieretti** vineyard en route (*p72*).

The distinctive La Pietra lighthouse in L'Île Rousse

The Best of the Rest

1. Plage de l'Ostriconi
D3

This sweep of golden sand and jade-green water is at the northwestern edge of the Désert des Agriate.

2. Nonza
E3 **Rte du Cap Corse, St Florent**

Pastel-painted houses and terraced gardens tumble down steep slopes in this village. Here, the church of St Julie, perched 160 m (524 ft) above a dark sand cove, is worth a visit.

3. Tour de Sénèque

Crowning the Cap Corse watershed, this remote tower makes a fine vantage point.

4. Boat Trips
F1 **San Paulu, Port de Plaisance, Macinaggio** **sanpaulu.fr**

This delightful two-hour trip cruises past the Îles Finocchiarola bird colony, making swimming stops at coves en route.

5. Corbara
C4

Corbara is famed for one of the island's most lavish Baroque churches, the Annonciation. The artifacts at the village's Musée Privé are also worth a look.

6. Lama
D4

As its grand period houses underline, Lama formerly ranked among the Balagne's most prosperous villages. It is now a quiet backwater albeit a very pretty one.

7. Algajola
B4

Packed around the western end of a broad, sandy beach, the pretty village of Algajola numbers among Corsica's most pleasant low-key seaside resorts.

8. Speloncato
C4

Extending to the distant sea, the view over the pale terra-cotta rooftops of Speloncato overlooking the green Regino Valley, is one of the most famous in the Balagne region.

9. Vallée du Fango
B6

The grandest of the valleys cutting into Corsica's interior from the Balagne coast, Fango ends abruptly at Paglia Orba's north face.

10. Galéria
B5

Galéria is the final outpost of Balagne before the coast road begins its long climb to the scenic Col de la Palmarella and Golfe de Porto. This remote fishing village is surrounded by several quiet beaches.

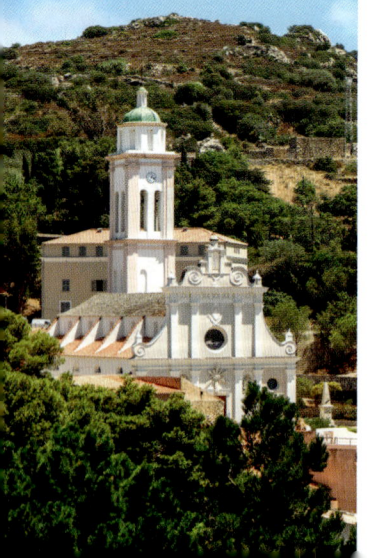

Baroque church of Annonciation, Corbara

Places to Eat

Patrons enjoying alfresco dining in Casa Musicale

1. Boutique Restaurant de Bastia

P5 4 Cnr Henri Pierangeli, Bastia terradicatoni.com · €€

An offshoot of the Terra di Catoni estate, this restaurant serves delicious local dishes.

2. I Salti

C4 Moulin de Salti, Speloncato 04953 43559 Mon; Nov–Apr · €€€

Dine on hearty regional cuisine in a lovely garden setting at this restaurant.

3. Le Pirate

F3 Erbalunga, Brando, 12 km (7 miles) N of Bastia Apr–Oct: noon–10pm Wed–Sun restaurant lepirate.com · €€€

The last word in gourmet Corsican seafood, Le Pirate also has a wine list that is second to none.

4. La Table Di Mà

B4 Hôtel A Casa Di Mà, Rte de Calvi, Lumio Nov–Apr acasa dima.com · €€€

High above the Golfe de Calvi in Lumio, this glitzy hotel-restaurant has a menu as enticing as the views.

5. Casa Musicale

C4 Pl de l'Église, Pigna Hours vary, check website casa-musicale. corsica · €€

Delicious food, made using locally sourced ingredients, is served here.

6. La Ferme de Campo di Monte

E4 Murato Hours vary, check website lafermedecampodimonte. fr · €€

Enjoy veal ragout and courgette fritters at this farmhouse hidden on a remote Nebbio mountainside. Reservations are essential.

7. U Arenacciu

E1 Barcaggio Port Hours vary, call ahead 04953 70239 · €€

This friendly local restaurant serves highlights from two globally loved cuisines: French and Italian. Expect fresh salads, lasagne and perfect pizzas.

8. La Roya

E3 Hotel de la Roya, Rte de la Plage, St-Florent Mon; Nov–early Apr hoteldelaroya.com · €€€

St-Florent's most elegant restaurant is in a modern four-star hotel. Dine on local seafood, salads and indulgent desserts, all with fine views of the bay.

9. Sampiero

P7 Pl du Donjon, Bastia 04953 22743 Hours vary, call ahead · €

A wide variety of seafood is on the menu at this restaurant, which is located close to the harbour.

10. Amama

D4 Cortaline, Lama 07494 78088 May–Oct: 9am–9pm daily; Nov–Apr: by reservation only · €€

Enjoy the views of Lama and live jazz in the evenings while feasting on wood-fired pizzas, charcuterie and the house speciality – crab penne.

STREETSMART

Signs in the village of Pigna

**CANTINA
A MORESCA**
· PETITE RESTAURATION DE TERROIR ·
CHARCUTERIE & FROMAGES FERMIERS
VINS DE PAYS & BIÈRES ARTISANALES
BOISSONS - GLACES

A CASARELLA
CAFÉ · RESTAURATION

**CASA
DI L'ARTIGIANI**

CASA MUSICALE
BAR · RESTAURANT · HOTEL

MERENDELLA
CHARCUTERIE - FROMAGE
BOISSONS

GETTING AROUND

Whether you're planning a multi-day hiking trip, a cycling tour, a coastal break or all of the above, here's all you need to know to navigate Corsica safely and efficiently.

PUBLIC TRANSPORT COSTS

BUS JOURNEY

€2.40

A single bus journey

TRAIN JOURNEY

€2

A single train ride

RAIL TRAVELCARD

€50

Unlimited rail travel for seven days

TOP TIP
Tickets can be bought from machines at most stations on the island.

SPEED LIMIT

HIGHWAYS

110 km/h (70 mph)

RURAL ROADS

90 km/h (55 mph)

URBAN AREAS

60 km/h (40 mph)

CAMPER-VANS

50 km/h (30 mph)

Arriving by Air

The island has four international airports: Calvi and Bastia in the north, and Figari Corse du Sud and Ajaccio in the south. Air Corsica (formerly CCM Airlines) flies from the island to many regions in France, including Aquitaine, Auvergne, Rhône-Alpes, Jura, Île-de-France, as well as Austria, Belgium, Italy, Portugal and Switzerland. Flights from European cities are less frequent in the winter months, when fewer passengers are looking to travel.

As the island's economy relies heavily on seasonal tourism, flight prices tend to be inflated in the summer months, with many visitors opting to arrive by sea from mainland France or Italy, instead.

Arriving by Sea

Corsica has direct sea connections with major Mediterranean ports in France, mainland Italy and the Italian island of Sardinia, with numerous year-round crossings assuring fast travel between these destinations. Sailings can be expensive, however, and fares fluctuate depending on the route. Both day and longer overnight ferry trips are available with most operators.

The island can be accessed by a 50-minute journey from Sante Teresa di Gallura in Sardinia. A boat to the Italian ports of Livorno, Savona, and Genoa, or Nice and Toulon in France take between 4.5–6 hours. The port of Marseille is reached in 9 hours. Trips carried out at night such as the crossing to Marseille with Corsica Linea can last around 12 hours.

Corsica Ferries are a popular choice for travel between the island, the mainland, Italy and the Italian island of Sardinia. **Corsica Linea** also has a range of options. If travelling between Corsica and Sardinia, **Ichnusa Lines** are worth exploring.
Corsica Ferries
w corsica-ferries.co.uk

Corsica Linea
🅦 corsicalinea.com/eng
Ichnusa Lines
🅦 ichnusalines.com/en

Boats and Cruises

Many of Corsica's best natural attractions are only reachable by sea. Corsica's seven main ports – Bastia, Calvi, Ajaccio, Bonifacio, Porto-Vecchio, L'Île-Rousse and Propriano – each offer regular short trips or day-long excursions, some with planned activities, guided coastal hikes or nature tours.

The best agencies include **Croisière Exclusive** in Porto- Vecchio and Ajaccio, **Calvi Evasion** in Calvi and **Corse Nautic Escape** in Bonifacio.
Calvi Evasion
🅦 calvi-evasion.com
Corsica Nautic
🅦 corsica-nautic.com
Corse Nautic Escape
🅦 corse-nautic-escape.com

Public Transport

Though the majority of visitors to the island bring their own car, a private vehicle is by no means essential when exploring Corsica. Many of the largest towns are served by bus and train, with the bus network extending to remote, mountainous destinations.

"U Trinighellu" (Little Train)

Train travel in Corsica may not be the fastest mode of transport, but it's among the most scenic. The most popular route on the island is known simply as "U Trinighellu" (the little train): a gondola mounted on tracks, it's small carriages make their way across the island's interior, with the main line running between Ajaccio, Corsica's capital, and Bastia, its second city. For more information on prices and timetables, you can visit the **Train Corse** website.
Train Corse
🅦 train-corse.com/fr/tarif-de-base

MAJOR FERRIES TO CORSICAN PORTS

Ferry Route	Distance	Weekly Crossings	Journey Time
Livorno - Bastia	130 km (80 miles)	5	5 hrs
Livorno - Ile Rousse	180 km (110 miles)	3	7 hrs
Toulon - Ajaccio	340 km (210 miles)	3	8 hrs
Toulon - Bastia	400 km (245 miles)	2	9 hrs
Toulon - Ile Rousse	300 km (185 miles)	2	8 hrs
Toulon - Porto Vecchio	410 km (255 miles)	2	15 hrs
Genoa - Bastia	200 km (125 miles)	5	6 hrs
Savona - Bastia	200 km (125 miles)	2	5 hrs
Savona - Ile Rousse	185 km (115 miles)	5	5 hrs
Santa Teresa di Gallura - Bonifacio	15 km (10 miles)	10	1 hr
Marseille - Ajaccio	400 km (250 miles)	6	10 hrs
Marseille - Porto Vecchio	475 km (300 miles)	4	14 hrs
Marseille - Propriano	430 km (265 miles)	4	13 hrs
Marseille - Ile Rousse	405 km (250 miles)	2	13 hrs
Nice - Bastia	260 km (160 miles)	4	5 hrs
Nice - Ile Rousse	215 km (135 miles)	3	5 hrs
Nice - Ajaccio	250 km (155 miles)	6	7 hrs
Nice - Porto Vecchio	320 km (200 miles)	2	13 hrs
Marseille - Bastia	450 km (285 miles)	3	10 hr
Piombino - Bastia	125 km (75 miles)	4	2.5 hrs
Portoferraio - Bastia	100 km (60 miles)	1	1.5 hrs
Porto Torres - Ajaccio	125 km (80 miles)	2	4 hrs

Other Trains

Chemin de Fer de la Corse (Corsican Rail) is a metre-gauge railway network that interconnects Corsica's four main towns: Calvi, Corte, Ajaccio and Bastia. The network is not extensive, only serving 16 stations across the island, but it's a great way of seeing the most popular tourist sights. One of the most frequented train stations is Vizzavona, which many visitors use as a departure point for the GR20 long-distance hiking path.

Note that ongoing efforts to modernize the railway network across the island mean some stations may be closed, even in the high season. For more information on rail travel on the island and for a full list of timetables, visit the **Corsican Rail** website.
Corsican Rail
📶 cf-corse.corsica/horaires

Bus Travel

Corsica's bus network provides a cheap and reliable way of navigating the island. Buses run between Bastia and Ajaccio (via Corte), Ajaccio and Porto Vecchio (via Sartène, Propriano, and Bonifacio), and Porto Vecchio and Bastia, with a connection to Macinaggio in Cap Corse. The island's bus operators also service several routes in Alta Rocca (in south Corsica) and the remote region of Porto.

The best place to consult frequently updated schedules and fares is on the **Corsica Bus** website. The island has various bus, mini-bus and coach operators – including **Autocars Corse-Méditerranée (ACM)**, **Muvistrada** and Eurocorse Voyages – and there is little integration between service routes, times or tickets, which can make long-distance bus travel something of a struggle.
Autocars Corse-Méditerranée
📶 autocarscorsemediterranee.fr
Corsica Bus
📶 corsicabus.org
Muvistrada
📶 mobilite.muvitarra.fr

Taxis

There are a number of taxi companies in most towns and villages across Corsica – most of their vehicles have a "Taxi" sign on the roof. Private taxi companies typically reveal journey prices on request. As with most forms of public transport on the island, prices are inflated during the busy tourist season. Popular options include **Taxi Yellow Cab** and **Taxi Porto Vecchio.**
Taxi Porto Vecchio
📶 taxi-portovecchio.com
Taxi Yellow Cab
📶 taxiyellowcabcorsica.com

Driving

The easiest and the most convenient way to get around Corsica is by car. Traveling on four wheels gives you access to the majority of the island's tourist attractions, as well as the freedom to plan your own adventures. Driving on the island is often an experience in itself, with some of France's most scenic roads.

Driving to Corsica

If you travel to the island in your vehicle, you will arrive in one of Corsica's seven passenger ferry ports (p175). The majority of ferry companies who make the crossing from mainland France, Italy or Sardinia also take personal vehicles for an extra charge.

Driving in Corsica

The Corsican roads are narrow and often exhiliratingly winding, except for the eastern T10 stretch that connects Bastia and Bonifacio. Navigating the precipitous zig-zags requires care and attention, as well as low driving speeds. Often, distances between destinations may seem short, but you are advised to leave ample time to navigate the treacherous roads. This should never be too much of an issue, as the island's twisting labyrinths offer some of the finest views.

In summer, the roads can become very congested, with long queues forming behind slow-moving coaches and tour buses. If at all possible, leaving your car and taking public transport is recommended in the height of the season.

Car Rental

Most of Europe's rental companies are found on the island, with agencies located at airports and in major towns and cities. To rent a car you must be 21 or over and have held a valid driver's licence for at least a year. Note that booking in advance gets you a better deal and ensures you get a car that will meet your needs.

Rules of the Road

The minimum driving age in France is 18, even if your licence qualifies you to drive at a younger age in your home country. Motorists in France drive on the right and overtake on the left. Traffic approaching from the right has priority at crossroads and junctions unless otherwise indicated. In heavy motorway traffic, vehicles are permitted to overtake on either side.

Cars must not enter an intersection in heavy traffic unless there's a clear path to exit the junction. Buses have priority when leaving stops and drivers must give way when one is signalling to re-join the carriageway (this applies in the UK, as well).

Using a mobile phone while driving can result in an immediate loss of licence. France strictly enforces a blood alcohol content limit of 0.05 per cent. Corsican police can demand on-the-spot payment of traffic fines, and drugs tests can be enforced even for minor infractions.

Cycling

Corsica's mountainous terrain offers some of the finest cycling in France, though the steep ascents and rapid descents demand experience, fitness and confidence.

Corsica's interior is a haven for mountain biking enthusiasts. Some stretches of the GR20 hiking trail can be adapted for off-road cycling, with routes leading down rugged mountains paths and through dense forests. The Grande Traversée (GT20 – the cyclist's equivalent of the GR20) crosses Corsica from north to south. Departing from Bastia and Cap Corse, the route reaches Bonifacio in 12 stages, taking in some of the island's best roads.

Bike Rental

There are a number of premium bike rental companies across Corsica. For the best road bikes, gravel bikes or e-bikes, **CCT Bike Rental** are a popular option. **BCyclet** offer bike rentals throughout Corsica and the French and Swiss Alps, with a particular focus on quality road bikes. For the best mountain bikes, bike shop **Wild Machja** in Calvi is a good choice.

BCyclet
🅦 bcyclet.com/bike-rental/corsica-bike-rental

CCT Bike Rental
🅦 cctbikerental.com

Wild Machja
🅦 wildmachja.com

Walking

Corsica is a hiker's paradise. Many hikers are aware of the notoriously challenging but richly rewarding GR20 long-distance route, which is among Europe's most popular hikes. The official **GR20** website has a wealth of information on walking the route. While this route is deservedly famous, the island is also home to a network of shorter mountain trails, undulating coastal walks and gentle forest strolls. The **Parc Naturel Régional de la Corse** (p44) maintains many of the island's best trails, and the park's website is an excellent resource for all sorts of hiking inspiration.

GR20
🅦 le-gr20.fr/en

Parc Naturel Régional de la Corse
🅦 pnr.corsica

PRACTICAL INFORMATION

A little local know-how goes a long way in Corsica. On these pages you can find all the essential advice and information you will need to make the most of your trip to this island.

AT A GLANCE

CURRENCY
Euro

AVERAGE DAILY SPEND

ON A BUDGET €65	MODERATE SPENDER €165	SPLASH OUT €300

BOTTLED WATER €2	COFFEE €3.50	BEER €7	DINNER FOR TWO €60

ESSENTIAL PHRASES

Hello	Bonjour
Goodbye	Au Revoir
Please	S'il vous plaît
Thank you	Merci
Do you speak English?	Parlez-vous anglais?
I don't understand	Je ne comprends pas

ELECTRICITY SUPPLY
Power sockets are type F, fitting two-pronged plugs. Standard voltage is 230v/50Hz.

Passports and Visas
For entry requirements, consult your nearest French embassy or check the **French-Visas** website. Citizens of the UK, US, Canada, Australia and New Zealand do not need a visa for stays of up to three months but in future must apply in advance for the European Travel Information and Authorization System (**ETIAS**); roll-out has often been postponed so check website for details.
ETIAS
W travel-europe.europa.eu/etias_en
French-Visas
W france-visas.gouv.fr

Government Advice
It is important to consult both your and the French government's advice before travelling. The U**K Foreign, Commonwealth and Development Office,** the **US State Department**, the **Australian Department of Foreign Affairs and Trade**, and French-Visas website *(above)* offer the latest information on security, health and local regulations.
Australian Department of Foreign Affairs and Trade
W smartraveller.gov.au
UK Foreign, Commonwealth and Development Office
W gov.uk/foreign-travel-advice
US State Department
W travel.state.gov

Customs Information
You can find information on laws relating to goods and currency taken in or out of France on the **Douanes and Droites Indirects** website.
Douanes and Droites Indirects
W douanes.gouv.frembassy
before departing.

Insurance
We recommend taking out a comprehensive insurance policy

covering medical care, theft, loss of belongings, cancellations and delays, and reading the small print carefully. UK citizens are eligible for free emergency medical care in France provided they have a valid European Health Insurance Card (EHIC) or UK Global Health Insurance Card (**GHIC**).

GHIC

w ghic.org.uk

Vaccinations
No vaccinations are required to visit Corsica.

Booking Accommodation
Corsica offers a wide range of accommodation, from five-star hotels to campsites (known as "refuges" along the GR20 route). Lodgings fill up quickly in the summer, particularly in Bonifacio and Ajaccio, so it's usually worth booking ahead.

Money
Corsica's currency is the euro. Major credit and debit cards are accepted by most businesses, while prepaid currency cards and American Express are accepted in some. Contactless payments are increasingly common, but it's always a good idea to carry some cash for smaller items, just in case. In rural areas, particularly if you are hiking the GR20, you may find smaller shops that do not take card.

Cash machines (ATMs) can be found everywhere. It is customary to tip between 5–10 per cent, and when buying a beer at a bar, by rounding up to the nearest euro.

Travellers With Specific Requirements
Visiting Corsica with specific requirements can be a tough task, particularly if you plan on leaving the larger towns. The terrain is steep and mountainous, and old villages typically have cobbled streets which may pose a challenge to wheelchair users. That said, many of the most beautiful attractions in and around Bonifacio and Ajaccio, including the beaches, are wheelchair accessible, and larger towns are generally well equipped for wheelchair users. Most ferries and boats from the mainland are also wheelchair accessible, though smaller boats to outlying islands may not be.

HandiOasis Corsica offers useful tips on accessible travel on the island. If visiting the Porto-Vecchio region, the **tourist board** has a handy website. Individual museum websites typically have a wealth of information on accessibility. Larger institutions are generally improving in their provisions for those with specific requirements.

HandiOasis Corsica

w handioasis-corsica.com

Porto-Vecchio Tourism

w portovecchio-tourisme.corsica/en/accessible-sites

Language
The official language is French, though many Corsicans also speak Italian. The standard of English varies, with fewer English speakers away from the main towns. In rural villages, you will often hear the Corsican language (Corsu) spoken – there are well over 200,000 native speakers and the language is thought to be growing again for the first time in decades.

Opening Hours
On Sundays, most rural shops are closed, and public transport services are typically reduced. Some museums and attractions and many restaurants are also closed for the day on Monday, particularly outside of the high season. Schools, post offices, shops and banks close on public holidays.

> Situations can change quickly and unexpectedly. Always check before visiting attractions and hospitality venues for up-to-date opening hours and booking requirements.

Personal Security

Corsica is generally a safe place for visitors, but it is always a good idea to take sensible precautions and be aware of your surroundings. Pickpockets are known to operate in busy tourist areas, particularly on public transport in larger towns and cities.

AT A GLANCE

EMERGENCY NUMBERS

EMERGENCY OPERATOR	POLICE
112	**17**

AMBULANCE	FIRE SERVICE
15	**18**

TIME ZONE
CET/CEST. Central European Summer Time runs from the last Sunday in March to the last Sunday in October.

TAP WATER
Unless stated otherwise, tap water is safe to drink.

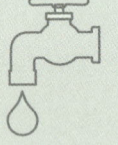

WEBSITES

France Tourism
Find inspiration and information on France's official tourism website (*france.fr*).

Visit Corsica
The official Corsican tourism website, (*visit-corsica.com*) has a wealth of information and ideas to help you make the most of your visit to the island.

Corsican Places
The Corsican Places website (*corsica.co.uk*) has advice on hotels.

If you have anything stolen, report the crime as soon as possible to the nearest police station. Get a copy of the crime report in order to claim on your insurance. Contact your embassy if you have your passport stolen, or in the event of a serious crime.

Corsicans are generally accepting of all people, regardless of their race, gender or sexuality. Same-sex marriage was officially legalized in France in 2013. In larger towns and cities like Ajaccio, you'll find dedicated LGBTQ+ nights, events and venues. Despite all the freedoms that the LGBTQ+ community enjoy, however, acceptance is not always a given, especially in more rural areas where locals may be unaccustomed to tourists. Rural Corsicans in particular are noted for their traditional outlook, but this rarely gives rise to hostility.

Health

France has a world-class health service. EU citizens are eligible to receive emergency medical treatment in France free of charge. If you have an EHIC or GHIC present this as soon as possible. For visitors from outside the EU, payment of medical expenses is the patient's responsibility. It is important to arrange comprehensive medical insurance before travelling.

Pharmacies are indicated by green crosses and can be used for help with minor ailments or prescriptions. You may need a doctor's prescription to obtain certain pharmaceuticals, and the pharmacist can inform you of the closest doctor's practice. Pharmacies are usually open 8am–6pm, and details of the nearest 24-hour service are posted in all pharmacy windows or can be found online.

For a serious illness or injury, visit a hospital or call an ambulance. In case of emergency, seek help in one of the island's medical institutions. Corsica has several hospitals providing good healthcare services and medical care to residents and visitors. Key establishments include Porto-Vecchio's Clinique de l'Ospedale, Sartène's Hospital U Spidali, Calvi's Centre Hospitalier Calvi Balagne and Bonifacio's Hospital de Bonifacio. All emergency rooms are part of the health system, so your EHIC, GHIC or insurance will cover you.

Smoking, Alcohol and Drugs

France has a smoking ban in all public places, including bars, cafés, restaurants and hotels. However, many establishments circumvent these laws. The possession of narcotics is prohibited and could result in prosecution and a prison sentence. Unless stated otherwise, it is permitted to drink alcohol on the streets and in public parks and gardens. France has a limit of 0.05 per cent BAC (blood alcohol content) for drivers.

ID

There is no requirement for visitors to carry ID, but in the event of a routine check you may be asked to show your passport. If you don't have it with you, the police may escort you to wherever your passport is being kept.

Local Customs

Etiquette is very important to Corsicans, just as it is to the French more generally. On entering and leaving a store, you are expected to say *"bonjour"* and *"au revoir"* to staff.

France has strict laws on hate speech. Disrespectful behaviour in public places can warrant a fine, or even prosecution.

Responsible Travel

Overtourism is having a stark impact on many of Corsica's most scenic spots, with crowds of tourists flocking to the scenic spots. This, coupled with the effects of climate change, can have serious environmental consequences. Ensure you stick to marked routes and refrain from swimming in forbidden spots. To offset the region's heavy traffic in summer, make use of the excellent public transport options and cycling paths. When hiking, always deposit rubbish in the available receptacles, or take it with you.

Mobile Phones and Wi-Fi

Visitors travelling to Corsica with EU tariffs can use their mobile phones abroad without being affected by data roaming charges; instead they will be charged the same rates for data, SMS and voice calls as they would pay at home. Visitors from other countries should check their contracts before using their phone in Corsica in order to avoid unexpected charges.

Post

Stamps (*timbres*) can be bought in post offices, newsagents, tobacconists and most major supermarkets. There are self-service stamp machines often conveniently placed outside larger post offices.

Taxes and Refunds

VAT is around 20 per cent in France. Non-EU residents are entitled to a tax refund subject to certain conditions. In order to obtain this, you must request a tax receipt and export papers when you purchase your goods. When leaving the country, present these papers, along with the receipt and your ID, at customs to receive your refund.

Discount Cards

Many towns and cities have a discount card giving cheaper access to public transport plus free or discounted admission to local attractions for a short period of time. These discounts and benefits are listed on individual town websites. For more information, visit the **Ajaccio** or **Bonifacio** websites – both of which are useful resources when in Corsica.

Ajaccio
w ajaccio-tourisme.com/en
Bonifacio
w bonifacio.co.uk

PLACES TO STAY

High-end hotels are in abundance across the island, many kitted out with the finest luxuries. Superb views of cream-coloured beaches, private plunge pools and palatial rooms – if you've got the budget, the sky's the limit. But if you know where to look, there are also some great bargains to be had, particularly in the numerous *gites d'étape* (refuges geared towards hikers). From renovated stables and humble hiking huts to epic luxury resorts, here's where to stay when exploring Corsica.

Bastia and the North

Relais International de la Jeunesse U Carabellu

🏠 Route de Pietra Maggiore, 20260 Calvi 🌐 clajsud.com/relais clajcalvi · €

This hostel might be one of the most affordable options in the Cap Corse vicinity, but it certainly doesn't cut corners. The views over the fort and bay are spectacular, the large dorm-style rooms are spacious and there are doubles for those looking for privacy, too. It's popular with hikers setting off on the GR20 (Calenzana is just a short drive away), particularly solo walkers looking to meet other intrepid hikers on their journey.

Aethos

🏠 Lieu Dit Paganacce, 20232 Oletta 🌐 aethos. com/corsica · €€€

Tucked away in the village of Oletta, in the hills between Bastia and St-Florent, Aethos has a claim to the best view on the island, with a sweeping panorama over the Gulf of St-Florent and its secluded bays. There's a wealth of rugged hiking trails on the doorstep, but the joys aren't confined to the world outside. Rooms are positively enormous, with interior decoration pulled straight from the pages of a design magazine.

La Villa Calvi

🏠 Chemin Notre Dame de la Serra, 20260 Calvi 🌐 lavilla.fr · €€€

Calvi's La Villa offers the pinnacle of Corsican luxury. Picture the scene: floating in the hotel's infinity pool with a glass of local wine, taking in the views over Calvi's citadelle. As well as rooms and suites, there are villas which sleep up to ten people, along with two bars, two restaurants and no fewer than four swimming pools. Rooms are minimalist with a seaside twist – think lamps made from driftwood and the like.

Camping Paduella

🏠 RN 197, 20260 Calvi 🌐 camping-paduella.com · €

This campsite must be doing something right to still be attracting clients almost 60 years after it first opened. Perhaps it's the pine trees that provide welcome shade in the height of summer, or maybe it's the sandy footpath that leads straight to the beach. No tent? No problem. There are also large ready-erected tents (generously referred to by the campsite as "bungalows"), which sleep between five and six people.

A Storia

🏠 3 Rue Marcel Paul, 20200 Bastia 🌐 astoriahotel.fr · €

This simple, no-frills accommodation is ideally positioned just across the street from Bastia's train station, and is under 10-minutes on foot from the old town, on the side of a very steep hill. The decor is rather dated, but the rooms are extremely spacious and there's plenty of on-site parking. The staff here are always willing to help with recommendations, so why not ask for some local advice as you tuck into a complementary French breakfast?

Hotel Castel Brando

🏠 Route du Cap Lieu-dit, 22222 Brando 🌐 castel brando.com · €€

In the gorgeous little fishing village of Erbalunga, Cap Corse, Hotel Castel Brando offers luxury in a truly peaceful setting. The hotel is backed by soaring mountains, with a palm-fronded swimming pool and a panoramic restaurant terrace. There's also a walled garden covered in creeping plants. The rooms are understated and painted in tasteful, earthy tones.

La Grotte des Naufragés

🏠 Calenzana region, address given upon reservation 🌐 closdu mouflon.fr/nuits-insolites-1 · €€

The "castaway's cave" offers an unforgettable stay. A small space naturally carved into the rock, the cave is perched above the sea and is accessed via a short hike through the maquis. Comfort takes second place here: the shower is outdoors, as is the bed,

and the toilet is dry composting. But sacrificing these home comforts is a small price to pay given the epic views, particularly at sunset.

La Caravelle

🏠 Route de la Plage, 20260 Calvi 🌐 hotel-la-caravelle.com · €€€

Just across the railway tracks from Calvi Beach, La Caravelle strips the luxury hotel back to basics. There are large rooms, many of which have their own terrace complete with sun loungers, and each with coffee machines and quality bathrobes. The on-site bar offers superb cocktails, and a sumptuous breakfast is served in the mornings. Note, however, that parking can be tricky – the public carpark opposite regularly fills up in season.

Marina d'Oro

🏠 Porte de Plaisance, 20248 Macinaggio 🌐 hotelmarinadoro.fr · €

This is one of a very small number of hotels in the remote Cap Corse, where self-catering is the default. Overlooking the pretty harbour of Macinaggio, Marina d'Oro puts you in a perfect position for hiking the legendary Sentier des Douaniers (Custom's Trail). Many of the rooms have sea views and spacious balconies; some even have two

large balconies per room. The rooms themselves are quaint and pretty, and the staff typically offer a warm welcome.

Corte and the Interior

Auberge de Jeunesse U Castellu

🏠 20172 Vero ☎ 0495 70 13 95 · €

Who says you can't do Corsica on a budget? This is one of the cheapest sleeps on the island, hidden in the wilderness just south of the village of Vero. Rooms are small and simple, but the main draw is the abundance of hiking right on the doorstep. Stock up on food before you arrive, as the nearest super-market is well over an hour's walk away.

Auberge du Col de Bavella

🏠 Place de la Fontaine, 20124 Bavella 🌐 auberge-bavella.com · €

In the heart of the Aiguilles de Bavella in the Corsican mountains, this retreat is revered by hikers tackling the GR20. For one thing, the restaurant serves up hearty Corsican fare in enormous portions. Looking for food on the go? Good value packed lunches are also available. The no-frills-attached dorm rooms sleep up to eight people, and there are private doubles.

Dominique Colonna

🏠 D623, Lieu-dit Restonica, 20250 Corte
🌐 dominique-colonna. com · €€

Just outside the town of Corte, this four-star hotel has a swimming pool, a small but well-equipped spa and a restaurant terrace suspended on decking over the river. The exposed stone walls and wooden shutters give a "back to nature" feel, but the best thing? The food is excellent, with an inventive array of Mediterranean dishes.

Bonifacio and the South

Les Bergeries de Palombaggia

🏠 Route de Palombaggia, 20137 Porto-Vecchio
🌐 hotel-palombaggia. com · €€€

These converted stables are camouflaged in the hills above Palombaggia beach, a crescent of golden sand that is often voted Corsica's best. This means it's a short stroll to the coast – but that's only if you're able to drag yourself from the hotel. Run by esteemed luxury brand Relais & Chateaux, this spot is fancy, with facilities including a large sea-facing infinity pool and two restaurants.

Cala di Greco

🏠 Bancarello, 20169 Bonifacio 🌐 hotel-caladigreco.com
· €€€

Cala di Greco is high-end,

with a hefty price point to match. Fork out and you'll be treated to some of the finest views over Bonifacio's citadelle, best admired from your own private jacuzzi. The hotel is shaded by maquis that gives it a feeling of total rural seclusion, and many of the huge rooms and spacious villas come with their own plunge pool. There's even an on-site gallery showcasing works by local artists.

Domaine de la Trinité

🏠 T40, 20169 Bonifacio
🌐 villas.versionmaquis. com · €€€

A rural haven, Domaine de la Trinité seems to blend effortlessly with the landscape, hidden between boulders and maquis. There are just two exclusive villas to rent: La Villa du Couvent, sleeping 10 people with a private heated pool, and Domaine de la Trinité, sleeping up to eight people, with private beach access. Few retreats are as luxurious as this.

Domaine de Sonia

🏠 U Pirellu Résidence, Route de Palombaggia, Porto-Vecchio 🌐 domaine desonia.com · €€

These eco "bubbles" (think transparent pods perched proudly on the hillside) are run solely on renewable energy. There are just three bubbles on-site, each equipped with an indoor shower, mini fridge and coffee

machine. You might feel as though you're in the middle of nowhere, but an array of conveniences are never far: meals and wine can be delivered to your bubble upon request, and the chefs scrimp on neither quality nor quantity.

Domaine de Peretti della Rocca

🏠 Pruno, 20114 Figari
🌐 deperettidella rocca.com · €€€

This spot is a true idyll for wine lovers, with rooms looking over the surrounding vineyards. There are rooms in the old stables as well as the main building, and a wooden cabin on stilts. Superb dining is available in the heart of the vines, with every dish carefully paired with a local vintage – the hardest part is choosing which wine to sample first.

Eastern Corsica

Camping Perla di Mare

🏠 Route de la Mer, 20240, Ghisonaccia 🌐 perla-di-mare.fr · €

One of the island's most popular camping complexes, Camping Perla di Mare runs a programme of summer activities, including pool parties, games nights, yoga classes and beach volleyball. There's a small pool, a kids' play area with sprinklers and games, and direct access to the beach. Whether you stay in a mobile home or a tent, there are few better spots for a family holiday.

La Plage CasadelMar

🏠 Presqu'île du Benedettu, 20137 Lecci 🌐 laplage casadelmar.fr · €€€

As you take a private boat trip out into the Gulf of Porto-Vecchio from the hotel's secluded pontoon, you'll understand what Corsican luxury is all about. This five-star hotel with enviable views and direct access to a private beach has long been a favourite with Corsica's wealthiest.

St Locavoile

🏠 Pore de Plaisance de Porto-Vecchio, 20137 Porto-Vecchio 🌐 stlocavoile.com · €

The sea has always been a defining feature of life on Corsica, so why not take to the waves for the night? St Locavoile is a sail boat that can be booked for short stays: the captain takes guests out to the Gulf of Porto-Vecchio before rowing back. Then it's just you and the waves.

Camping Bagheera

🏠 Bagheera, 20230 Bravone 🌐 bagheera.fr · €€

Southeast Corsica has a big naturist scene, with whole resorts dedicated to taking your kit off. Want to give it a try? Camping Bagheera offers direct access to a popular nudist beach.

Some light clothing is recommended for the restaurants and gym; otherwise your birthday suit will suffice.

Ajaccio and the West Coast

Les Flots Bleus, Porto

🏠 Porto Marine, 20150 Ota 🌐 hotel-lesflotsbleus.com · €€

Here, it's all about the view. Every room looks due west over the sea, and each is equipped with a large balcony from which to take it in. And when you're done swooning over the sea from a distance, Porto's port, with boat trips to nearby Girolata and Scandola, is just a five-minute walk away.

E Casarelle

🏠 Vignarella, 20147 Osani 🌐 ecasarelle.wixsite.com · €

Found on the fringes of Scandola, Corsica's only UNESCO-listed reserve, the little hamlet of Girolata is only reachable by boat or on foot. Here, cows roam freely on the beach, significantly outnumbering people. With four bungalows, E Casarelle is a humble but homely place to stay.

Tour de Micalona

🏠 20113 Olmeto 🌐 domaine-de-logliastru.com · €€€

Like something from a fairytale, this luxury accommodation is found in an old Genoese watch-tower. It sits in complete solitude by the coast, looking somewhat foreboding on approach. Get closer, however, and a world of luxury awaits: there's a jacuzzi and a swimming pool carved into the rock, along with circular stone-walled bedrooms. You've never stayed anywhere like this.

Funtana a l'Ora

🏠 Il Campo, 20150 Ota 🌐 funtanaalora.fr · €

Funtana a l'Ora is all about stripping life back to the essentials. Tent pitches, mobile homes and chalets are tucked between the mountains and the sea, and you can choose from a heated pool or a chilly river fed by waterfalls for a dip. When you're done exploring, the on-site pizzeria is great value.

Cala di Sole, Ajaccio

🏠 5 Route des Îles Sanguinaires, 20000 Ajaccio 🌐 caladisole.fr · €€

Love the outdoors, but reluctant to leave the convenience of the city? Cala di Sole offers the best of both worlds: a 15-minute drive from Ajaccio, it's halfway between the city and the verdant La Parata headland, which looks over the islets off the Corsican coast. There's a small restaurant with sea views (closed every Tuesday) and a small cocktail bar on-site.

INDEX

Page numbers in **bold** refer to main entries.

PHRASE BOOK

In Emergency

Help!	Au secours!	oh se*koor*
Stop!	Arrêtez!	aret-*ay*
Call a doctor!	Appelez un médecin!	apuh-*lay* uñ medsañ
Call an ambulance!	Appelez une ambulance!	apuh-*lay* oon oñboo-*loñs*
Call the police!	Appelez la police!	apuh-*lay* lah poh-*lees*
Call the fire brigade!	Appelez les pompiers!	apuh-*lay* leh poñ-*peeyay*
Where is the nearest telephone?	Où est le téléphone le plus proche?	oo ay luh tehleh*fon* luh ploo prosh
Where is the nearest hospital?	Où est l'hôpital le plus proche?	oo ay l'*opeetal* luh ploo prosh

Communication Essentials

Yes	Oui	wee
No	Non	noñ
Please	S'il vous plaît	seel voo *play*
Thank you	Merci	mer-*see*
Excuse me	Excusez-moi	exkoo-*zay* mwah
Hello	Bonjour	boñzhoor
Goodbye	Au revoir	oh ruh-*vwar*
Good evening	Bonsoir	boñ-*swar*
Morning	Le matin	matañ
Afternoon	L'après-midi	l'apreh-*meedee*
Evening	Le soir	swar
Yesterday	Hier	eeyehr
Today	Aujourd'hui	oh-zhoor-*dwee*
Tomorrow	Demain	duhmañ
Here	Ici	ee-*see*
There	Là	lah
What?	Quel, quelle?	kel, kel
When?	Quand?	koñ
Why?	Pourquoi?	poor-*kwah*
Where?	Où?	oo

Useful Phrases

How are you?	Comment allez-vous?	kom-*moñ* ta*lay voo*
Very well, thank you.	Très bien, merci.	treh byañ, mer-*see*
Pleased to meet you.	Enchanté de faire votre connaissance.	oñshoñ-*tay* duh fehr votr kon-ay-*sans*
See you soon.	À bientôt.	abyañ-*toh*
That's fine.	Voilà qui est parfait.	vwalah kee ay parfay
Where is/are…?	Où est/sont…?	oo ay/soñ
How far is it to…?	Combien de kilomètres d'ici à…?	kom-*byañ* duh is keelo-*metr* d'ee-see ah
Which way to…?	Quelle est la direction pour…?	kel ay lah *deer*-ek-syoñ poor
Do you speak English?	Parlez-vous anglais?	par-*lay* voo oñg-*lay*
I don't understand.	Je ne comprends pas.	zhuh nuh kom-*proñ* pah
Could you speak slowly, please?	Pouvez-vous parler moins vite, s'il vous plaît?	poo-*vay* voo par-*lay* mwañ veet see voo play
I'm sorry.	Excusez-moi.	exkoo-*zay* mwah

Useful Words

big	grand	groñ
small	petit	puh-*tee*
hot	chaud	show
cold	froid	frwah
good	bon	boñ
bad	mauvais	moh-*veh*
enough	assez	assay
well	bien	byañ
open	ouvert	oo-*ver*
closed	fermé	fer-*meh*
left	gauche	gohsh
right	droite	drwaht
straight on	tout droit	too drwah
near	près	preh
far	loin	lwañ
up	en haut	oñ oh
down	en bas	oñ *bah*
early	de bonne heure	duh bon *urr*
late	en retard	oñ ruh-*tar*
entrance	l'entrée	l'oñ-*tray*
exit	la sortie	sor-*tee*
toilet	les toilettes, les WC	twah-*let*, vay-*see*
unoccupied	libre	leebr
no charge	gratuit	grah-*twee*

Shopping

How much does this cost?	C'est combien s'il vous plaît?	say kom-*byañ* seel voo play
Do you take credit cards?	Est-ce que vous acceptez les cartes de crédit?	es-*kuh* voo zaksept-*ay* leh kart duh kreh-*dee*
I would like …	Je voudrais…	zhuh voo-*dray*
Do you have?	Est-ce que vous avez?	es-*kuh* voo zavay
I'm just looking.	Je regarde seulement.	zhuh ruhgar suhl*moñ*
What time do you open?	A quelle heure vous êtes ouvert?	ah kel urr voo zet oo-*ver*
What time do you close?	A quelle heure vous êtes fermé?	ah kel urr voo zet fer-*may*
This one	Celui-ci	suhl-wee-*see*
That one	Celui-là	suhl-wee-*lah*
expensive	cher	shehr
cheap	pas cher, bon marché	pah shehr, boñ mar-*shay*

Types of Shop

antique shop	le magasin d'antiquités	maga-*zañ* d'oñteekee-*tay*
bakery	la boulangerie	booloñ-*zhuree*
bank	la banque	boñk
book shop	la librairie	lee-brehree
butcher	la boucherie	boo-*shehree*
cake shop	la pâtisserie	patee-*sree*
cheese shop	la fromagerie	fromazh-*ree*
chemist	la pharmacie	farmah-*see*
dairy	la crémerie	krem-*ree*
department store	le grand magasin	groñ maga-*zañ*
delicatessen	la charcuterie	sharkoot-*ree*
fishmonger	la poissonnerie	pwasson-*ree*
gift shop	le magasin de cadeaux	maga-*zañ* duh kadoh
greengrocer	le marchand de légumes	mar-*shoñ* duh lay-*goom*
grocery	l'alimentation	alee-moñta-*syoñ*
hairdresser	le coiffeur	kwafuhr
market	le marché	marsh-*ay*
newsagent	le magasin de journaux	maga-*zañ* duh zhoor-*no*
post office	la poste, le bureau de poste, les PTT	pohst, booroh duh pohst, peh-teh-teh
shoe shop	le magasin de chaussures	maga-*zañ* duh show-*soor*
supermarket	le supermarché	soo pehr-*marshay*
tobacconist	le tabac	tabah
travel agent	l'agence de voyages	l'azhoñs duh vwayazh

Eating Out

Have you got a table?	Avez-vous une table libre?	avay-**voo** oon tahbl leebr
I want to reserve a table.	Je voudrais réserver une table.	zhuh voo-**dray** rayzehr-**vay** oon tahbl
the bill, please.	L'addition, s'il vous plaît.	l'adee-**syoñ** seel voo **play**
I am a vegetarian.	Je suis végétarien.	zhuh swee vezhay-**tehryañ**
Waitress Waiter	Madame, Mademoiselle/ Monsieur	mah-**dam**, mah-dem wah **zel**/muh-**syuh**
menu	le menu, la carte	men-**oo**, kart
fixed-price menu	le menu à prix fixe	men-**oo** ah pree feeks
cover charge	le couvert	koo-**vehr**
wine list	la carte des vins	kart-**deh vañ**
glass	le verre	vehr
bottle	la bouteille	boo-**tay**
knife	le couteau	koo-**toh**
fork	la fourchette	for-**shet**
spoon	la cuillère	kwee-**yehr**
breakfast	le petit déjeuner	puh-**tee** deh-**zhuh-nay**
lunch	le déjeuner	deh-**zhuh-nay**
dinner	le dîner	dee-**nay**
main course	le plat principal	plah prañsee-**pal**
starter, first course	l'entrée, le hors d'oeuvre	l'oñ-**tray**, or-duhvr
dish of the day	le plat du jour	plah doo zhoor
wine bar	le bar à vin	bar ah vañ
café	le café	ka-**fay**
rare	saignant	say-**noñ**
medium	à point	ah **pwañ**
well done	bien cuit	byañ **kwee**

Menu Decoder

l'agneau	l'anyoh	lamb
l'ail	l'eye	garlic
la banane	banan	banana
le beurre	burr	butter
la bière	bee-**yehr**	beer
le bifteck, le steak	beef-tek, stek	steak
le boeuf	buhf	beef
bouilli	boo-yee	boiled
le café	kah-**fay**	coffee
le canard	kanar	duck
le citron pressé	see-troñ press-**eh**	fresh lemon juice
les crevettes	kruh-vet	prawns
les crustacés	kroos-ta-**say**	shellfish
cuit au four	kweet oh foor	baked
le dessert	deh-ser	dessert
l'eau minérale	l'oh meeney-ral	mineral water
les escargots	leh zes-kar-goh	snails
les frites	freet	chips
le fromage	from-azh	cheese
les fruits frais	frwee freh fresh	fruit
les fruits de mer	frwee duh mer	seafood
le gâteau	gah-toh	cake
la glace	glas	ice, ice cream
grillé	gree-yay	grilled
le homard	omahr	lobster
l'huile	l'weel	oil
le jambon	zhoñ-boñ	ham
le lait	leh	milk
les légumes	lay-goom	vegetables
la moutarde	moo-tard	mustard
l'oeuf	l'uf	egg
les oignons	leh zonyoñ	onions
les olives	loh zoleev	olives
l'orange pressée	l'oroñzh press-eh	fresh orange juice
le pain	pan	bread
le petit pain	puh-tee pañ	roll
poché	posh-ay	poached
le poisson	pwah-**ssoñ**	fish
le poivre	pwavr	pepper
la pomme	pom	apple
les pommes de terre	pom-duh tehr	potatoes
le porc	por	pork
le potage	poh-**tazh**	soup
le poulet	poo-lay	chicken
le riz	ree	rice
rôti	row-tee	roast
la sauce	sohs	sauce
la saucisse	sohsees	sausage, fresh
sec	sek	dry
le sel	sel	salt
le sucre	sookr	sugar
le thé	tay	tea
le toast	toast	toast
la viande	vee-yand	meat
le vin blanc	vañ bloñ	white wine
le vin rouge	vañ roozh	red wine
le vinaigre	veenaygr	vinegar

Staying in a Hotel

Do you have a vacant room?	Est-ce que vous avez une chambre?	es-kuh voo-**zavay** oon shambr
double room	la chambre pour deux	shambr pehr duh
with double bed	la chambre à personnes, avec un grand lit	shambr ah pehr-son, avek un groñn lee
twin room	la chambre à deux lits	shambr ah duh lee
single room	la chambre pour une personne	shambr ah oon pehr-son
room with a bath, shower	la chambre avec salle de bains, une douche	shambr avek sal duh bañ, oon doosh
porter	le garçon	gar-**soñ**
key	la clef	klay
I have a reservation.	J'ai fait une réservation.	zhay fay oon rayzehrva-**syoñ**

Sightseeing

abbey	l'abbaye	l'abay-ee
art gallery	la galerie d'art	galer-ree dart
cathedral	la cathédrale	katay-dral
church	l'église	l'aygleez
garden	le jardin	zhar-dañ
library	la bibliothèque	beebleeo-tek
museum	le musée	moo-zay
railway station	la gare (SNCF)	gahr (es-en-say-ef)
bus station	la gare routière	gahr roo-tee-yehr
tourist information office	les renseignements touristiques, le syndicat d'initiative	roñsayn-moñ too-rees-teek, sandee-ka d'eenee-syateev
town hall	l'hôtel de ville	l'ohtel duh veel
private mansion	l'hôtel particulier	l'ohtel partikoo-lyay
closed for public holiday	fermeture jour férié	fehrmeh-tur zhoor fehree-ay

Numbers

00	zéro	zeh-roh
01	un, une	uñ, oon
02	deux	duh
03	trois	trwah
04	quatre	katr
05	cinq	sañk
06	six	sees
07	sept	set
08	huit	weet
09	neuf	nerf
10	dix	dees
11	onze	oñz
12	douze	dooz

ACKNOWLEDGMENTS

This edition updated by

Contributors Anna Richards, Robin Gauldie

Senior Editor Alison McGill

Senior Designers Stuti Tiwari, Laura O'Brien

Project Editor Alex Pathe

Art Editor Sulagna Das

Assistant Editor Abhidha Lakhera

Proofreader Stephanie Smith

Indexer Rhiannon Thomas

Picture Research Deputy Manager
Virien Chopra

Assistant Picture Research Administrator
Manpreet Kaur

Senior Picture Researcher Nishwan Rasool

Publishing Assistant Simona Velikova

Jacket Designer Laura O'Brien

Senior Cartographic Editor James Macdonald

Cartography Manager Suresh Kumar

Project Cartographer Ashif Ashif

Senior DTP Designer Rohit Rojal

Senior Production Controller Samantha Cross

Managing Editor Beverly Smart

Managing Art Editor Gemma Doyle

Senior Managing Art Editor Priyanka Thakur

Art Director Maxine Pedliham

Editorial Director Hollie Teague

Publishing Director Georgina Dee

DK would like to thank the following for their
contribution to the previous editions: Richard
Abram, Dana Facaros

The publisher would like to thank the following
for their kind permission to reproduce their
photographs:

Key: a-above; b-below/bottom; c-center; f-far;
l-left; r-right; t-top

Adobe Stock: Dynamoland 31b, Alexandre Rosa
26cra, A. Zeitler 21tr, 29br, ZoltanJozsef 43b

Alamy Stock Photo: Abaca Press 74t, Shootpix
/ Abacapress.com 76b, Blickwinkel / P. Royer 59,
68, Pascal Boegli 63t, Chronicle 10tr, 10cla,
Antoine Durand 15t, EYESITE 85, foxy726 13tl,
Julia Gavin 61b, Hemis / Bertrand Gardel 20cl,
84b, Brusini Aurélien / Hemis.fr 13clb, Guiziou

Franck / Hemis.fr 84t, Lansard Gilles / Hemis.fr
13cl (8), 16crb, 50-51, 58, Lemaire Stéphane /
Hemis.fr 15cla, 16tl, 101, Moirenc Camille /
Hemis.fr 72b, 102b, Montico Lionel / Hemis.fr 1
89, Rieger Bertrand / Hemis.fr 9tr, 13cl, 87,
Heritage Image Partnership Ltd 8, Image
Professionals GmbH / Ginet -Drin / Photocuisir
71b, Image Professionals GmbH / LOOK-foto 1
Image Professionals GmbH / TravelCollection 3
imageBROKER / Daniel Schoenen 92,
imageBROKER / Raimund Franken 40-41b, 49,
imageBROKER.com GmbH & Co. KG / Arco / F.
Schneider 90b, imageBROKER.com GmbH & Co
KG / Erhard Nerger 46b, imageBROKER.com
GmbH & Co. KG / Mara Brandl 63b,
incamerastock / ICP 9tl, Jon Arnold Images Ltd /
Walter Bibikow 13bl, 54b, 107, Joana Kruse 104,
Jonathan Little 70, mauritius images GmbH /
Rainer Mirau 103b, NielsVK 35tr, 41t, Loic
Colonna / Onlyfrance.fr 47, Robert Palomba /
Onlyfrance.fr 69, Stephane FRANCES /
Onlyfrance.fr 105, Penta Springs Limited 9br,
Realy Easy Star 9cr, Sergi Reboredo 66, Dirk
Renckhoff 32b, robertharding / David Tomlinsor
36b, David Robertson 86, Raphael Salzedo 77,
Witold Skrypczak 57b, 96-97b, Antony Souter 67
StockShot / John Wilhelmsson 61t, The Print
Collector / Heritage Images 10tl, Markus
Thomenius 93, Truxtman 26-27b, Westend61 60
Westend61 GmbH 13cla, Westend61 GmbH /
Manuel Sulzer 82t, Jan Wlodarczyk 38, 82-83b

AWL Images: Walter Bibikow 23b, 79, Davide
Camesasca 45, ClickAlps 6-7, 16tr, Hemis 35tl,
Francesco Riccardo Iacomino 1, 5, 34-35b

Depositphotos Inc: sam741002 57t

Le DIAN'ARTE Museum: 33b

Dreamstime.com: Allard1 21cr, Richard Banary
98, Dorinmarius 14, Eugenesergeev 11b,
Giuseppe De Filippo 29cb, Jon Ingall 12cr, 15cra,
28, 29bl, 37b, 46t, 62, 96t, Vadym Lavra 42-43t,
Tom Meaker 65b, Morseicinque 64b, Olezzo 95,
Sam74100 56, Vampy1 35cra, Jeff Whyte 22b

Getty Images: Pierre Berlioz / 500px 12br, AFP /
- / Stringer 11t, AFP / Francois Desjobert / - /
Stringer 10clb, Pascal Pochard-Casabianca / AFP
76t, Corbis Documentary / Maremagnum 81,
DigitalVision / Walter Bibikow 53, Moment /
Marius Roman 90t, Photodisc / Alex Treadway
12crb, 91, Stockbyte Unreleased / Guido Cozzi /
Atlantide Phototravel 35ca, The Image Bank
Unreleased / Marc Dozier 48, Universal Images
Group / Education Images 64t

A NOTE FROM DK

The rate at which the world is changing
is constantly keeping the DK travel team
on our toes. While we've worked hard to
ensure that this edition of Top Ten Corsica is
accurate and up-to-date, we know that
opening hours alter, standards shift, prices
fluctuate, places close and new ones pop up in
their stead. So, if you notice we've got
something wrong or left something out, we
want to hear about it. Please get in touch at
travelguides@dk.com

Within each Top 10 list in this book,
no hierarchy of quality or popularity is
implied. All 10 are, in the editor's opinion,
of roughly equal merit.

First edition 2012

Published in Great Britain by Dorling
Kindersley Limited, DK, 20 Vauxhall Bridge Road,
London SW1V 2SA

The authorised representative in the EEA is
Dorling Kindersley Verlag GmbH. Arnulfstr.
124, 80636 Munich, Germany

Published in the United States by DK Publishing,
1745 Broadway, 20th Floor, New York, NY 10019, USA

Copyright © 2012, 2025 Dorling Kindersley Limited
A Penguin Random House Company

25 26 27 28 10 9 8 7 6 5 4 3 2 1

The publishers cannot accept responsibility for any consequences
arising from the use of this book, nor for any material on third
party websites, and cannot guarantee that any website address in
this book will be a suitable source of travel information.

A CIP catalog record for this book
is available from the British Library.

A catalog record for this book is available
from the Library of Congress.

ISSN: 1542 1554
ISBN: 978 0 2417 3512 1

Printed and bound in China

www.dk.com

MIX
Paper | Supporting
responsible forestry
FSC™ C018179

This book was made with Forest
Stewardship Council™ certified
paper – one small step in DK's
commitment to a sustainable future.
Learn more at **www.dk.com/uk/
information/sustainability**